Poker Strategy

Books By
A.D. Livingston

Poker Strategy

Proven Principles for Winning Play

A.D. Livingston

THE LYONS PRESS
Guilford, Connecticut
An imprint of The Globe Pequot Press

The Lyons Press is an imprint of The Globe Pequot Press.

10 9 8 7 6 5 4 3 2 1

Printed in Canada

ISBN 1-59228-352-7

Library of Congress Cataloging-in-Publication Data is available on file.

Introduction

The first edition of *Poker Strategy and Winning Play* came out 20 years ago. At that time, I had recently published an article in *Life* magazine about a new game, which, I predicted, would replace five-card stud as the the major big-money poker game for the rest of the 20th Century. I was right. Now called Hold 'em, or Texas Hold 'em, the game is dealt in the annual world championship poker tournaments in Las Vegas and in big money games elsewhere. Since my prediction has come true, perhaps the reader will permit me to say that the book is more clearly relevant to poker today than it was at the time of first publication.

I feel also that the modern reader can more easily take advantage of the mathematical section of the book. Believe it or not, I worked out the probability figures with a slide rule, then ran the formulas through a calculator for 3-digit accuracy. This wasn't a shirt pocket electronic calculator, nor even a desktop calculator. I literally cranked the numbers out with a mechanical device that was, at the time, made in Germany. It's hard to believe that within a mere twenty-year span the electronic calculator has become so widespread, so powerful, and so cheap. Twenty years. How the times have changed. Yet, the basic mathematics of poker have not changed, and modern technology merely makes the odds easier to figure. Of course, knowing how to figure the odds will not make a winning player. But a total disregard of the odds for a long period of play will surely make a loser. Lucky players don't last.

Other than this new introduction, the major change made in the new edition is the deletion of a list of books about poker and related topics. Books come and go, it seems, and I am indeed fortunate that my publisher is giving a new lease of life to *Poker Strategy and Winning Play*. Am I lucky—or is the book that good? You'll have to decide that one for yourself.

Before closing, I would like to say a somewhat whimsical word or two about the trends in my writing career. My first three books were about poker and gambling. My next four were about bass fishing. A strange mixture? Maybe not. The two topics seem to be related (especially in the requirement of patience to insure success) and poker is not unknown in many fishing and hunting camps. As the late Jason Lucas said, "Fishing and poker are analogous: one has to become quite good at either to realize that, in comparing one man's 'take' with another's, the element of luck is almost nonexistent; the expert nearly always gets more. There are times when even the best bass angler cannot discover bass that are feeding, and times when even the slickest professional gambler cannot find his suckers. But there is hardly a day when the real adept at either cannot at least do well enough for eating purposes." Is it then mere coincidence that my last three books should be about foods and cooking?

A. D. LIVINGSTON
June, 1991

Preface
(for losers only)

My father once told me that he quit playing poker because he liked the game too much. It will be obvious to anyone reading this book that I too like poker. It will also be obvious that I have not followed my father's example!

Although I have not made an obsession of poker, I have certainly taken it more seriously than a harmless pastime. The plain truth is that poker is not a harmless pastime, unless one limits his action to an occasional penny ante party. Poker—real poker—is either profitable or costly, since one man's gain has got to be another man's loss.

I therefore advise each loser among the 50 million Americans who play at poker to either quit the game or become a winner. Because anyone reading this book evidently has no immediate intentions of giving up the game, we can get on with the alternative. Playing a winning game of poker is what this book is about. The basics, the principles, and the higher strategy set forth in Part One apply to any game that can be called poker. Part Two deals with the mathematics of the game, presenting first theory and then handy tables. Part Three, arranged alphabetically, covers dozens of dealer's choice games, such as Seven-Card Stud, Deuces Wild, and Cincinnati.

I hope that the reader will find the book easy going the first time through and easy to use as a reference in the years to come.

A. D. LIVINGSTON

Timucaun Island, Lake Weir
Summerfield, Florida
April, 1971

Contents

PART THREE: DEALER'S CHOICE

(Games are discussed in alphabetical order in text. Only the principal ones are listed here.)

I have often wondered if the results of the Versailles Conferences following the First World War would have been different if Woodrow Wilson had been a poker player.

—CLYDE BRION DAVIS

Part One

Strategy and Principles

1.

Conducting a Poker Game

The steadfast players with regular seats in an unusually tough poker game sharpened their shears whenever a certain lamb sat in. Competition for the easy money ran high. One night, while the fumble-fingered guy was sitting on my immediate right, he flashed his cards so often that it was all but impossible for me not to glimpse a red ace or a black king from time to time. I was probably feeling a little guilty about taking the guy's money, so I asked him to please watch his cards. I asked him more than once. But he kept flashing them until finally a hardrock player across the table (who hadn't yet fleeced the lamb) said, "Hold your goddamn cards down, fellow. Livingston can see your hand—and that gives him an advantage over *me!*"

Indeed it did. But I would have had even more advantage if the lamb had been on my left. Why? Not only because he opened the pot freely but also because he bet or called or raised or folded out of turn. If he had been on my left I would have known, half the time, what he intended to do before I acted on my hand. But, since he sat on my right, this information was seldom of value to me, and his folding out of turn, or raising out of turn, often influenced what action the other players took on my bets and raises.

If, for example, I made a full house and bet $5, another player around the board would probably have seen me on two pairs if the lamb had not called out of turn. Another example: A player across the board opened in Jacks. The lamb called. I called. The opener drew two cards, apparently to triplets. The lamb drew one. I drew two, holding small triplets. As soon as the lamb looked at his draw card, he threw in his hand *before the opener acted.* No longer concerned about a flush, the opener bet into me. If he did not fill up, he may have checked (and my seeing his high triplets wouldn't have cost me a cent) if the lamb had not acted out of turn.

The examples given above are not at all unusual in social games. At least 90 percent of the poker sessions would be fairer to all players and would proceed smoother if everyone would learn to ante, bet, check, raise, call, and fold in turn. It's difficult to enforce "laws" about this sort of thing, and I think that acting on your hand only when it's your turn to act is as much a matter of ethics and etiquette as of law. It is a common courtesy to other players.

Actually, there are no laws for poker. Hoyle died fifty years before poker was invented. Several other people have drafted excellent sets of poker laws, but unfortunately there is no officiating organization to enforce them. On the other hand, every card game, and especially a money game like poker, must be played by rules. What it boils down to is that each private game and each public or house game must decide on its own laws. It is the responsibility of each individual player to know and understand these laws, and to see that they are carried out. Most groups could eliminate much debate at the table if they would take out time enough to write the laws down.

Agreeing on a set of laws for a particular group would be fairly easy. It's simply a matter of getting the players together on certain points. But drafting a set of "universal" poker laws would present any number of insoluble problems. To check and raise, for example, is perfectly acceptable poker in one group, but in another it may be offense enough to incite a duel. Personally, I feel that it is no more unethical to check a lock than to bet into a man after he has shown weakness by checking. I like the check and raise game because it gives more range for strategy and positional jockeying. Yet, if I play with a group that frowns upon such sandbagging, I certainly respect their codes.

Frankly, I doubt that any set of laws can apply without exceptions to all poker groups. The public poker houses of California have special rules that, however necessary from a business or public relations viewpoint, are detrimental to higher poker strategy. I can see why a house would have such rules, but I see no need for private groups to abide by them. Nor do I see any reason why a private group should necessarily abide by the "official" laws published in a book. Too many published laws are open to question, and no book of rules can keep up, in any detail, with new dealer's choice games. Even some of the old problems, such as splitting openers, have not been solved, or at least no "solution" has gained anything like universal acceptance.

Even if a poker group adopts a set of published laws, the players will still have to make many decisions for themselves. The check and raise problem is a good example. The United States Playing Card Company has been publishing rules on card games since the latter 1800's, but they haven't taken a firm stand on the check and raise issue, as the following quote from one of their booklets shows: "In general a bet is unwise when some other player has taken the lead against you; it is better to check (*if the rules allow*) and let him bet, whereupon you can raise." The italics in the parenthetical clause are mine.

So . . . forget it if you are looking for a set of printed rules that will be the law in every poker game in the land. Still, each group would profit by having a set of printed laws to use as guidelines. Several of the Hoyle books have reasonably good laws, but I recommend those published in *Official Rules of Card Games* by the United States Playing Card Company. This paperback sells for only $1.00, so that each member of a poker group can easily afford to own one. Why not chip the pot and order a copy for everybody? The address: The United States Playing Card Company, P.O. Box 12126, Cincinnati, Ohio 45212. Better yet, place the order through your local book dealer.

♥ ♥ ♥

In addition to having a set of rules and playing by them, a number of other gentlemanly practices will make a poker game go smoother from hour to hour and will help hold it together from Friday night to Friday night, week by week, year after year. Here are some suggestions:

1. Set a time limit and stick to it. The aftermath often hurts more poker players financially than the session itself does. Playing all night not only reduces a man's efficiency on his job the next day but also threatens his home life and ruins his health. I like to have the right to quit at any time, winners or losers. But in some social groups it is good form to play until quitting time comes.

2. Insist that the players arrive on time. If a player habitually comes late, stop inviting him. Sure, everybody would like to drop by at his own convenience—but somebody has to be there to get the game kicked off.

3. More and more poker circles are letting the dealer ante for everybody. If the ante is prorated at 25¢ per player and there are eight players, the dealer puts in $2. This averages out, is fair for everyone, keeps the pot right, and helps the players remember whose turn it is to deal. In general, this method of anteing makes for a smoother and faster poker session. The only problem with it is that it may be desirable to vary the ante with stud and draw games in a dealer's choice session. Many players prefer a larger ante for draw. In this case, the dealer makes the regular ante and calls for additional ante from all players (including himself).

4. Play with cash, or with chips that are backed by cash, in any game above penny ante. Never play IOU's or checks in a pot or in a chip bank. Any player who wants to borrow money or get a check cashed should put it on a personal basis, man to man, with another player. That way, only whoever agrees to cash the check or make the loan gets stuck with bad paper or debt. Never transfer debts from one player to another, no matter how good a bookkeeper you are! Never let debts accumulate over a period of weeks; settle all debts from one session before you start another.

5. Using chips instead of cash will speed up a game. They are easier to manage and count.

6. In many circles, any player can cut the deck at any time he has a hunch to do so, no matter what the rulebooks say. But the right to cut the deck is so often abused in some circles that "there ought to be a law against it." Once started, players sometimes cut, and cut another's cut, so often that it slows down the play considerably. This happened in a game I used to frequent in Huntsville, Alabama. The solution was to allow anyone to cut the cards at any time *if* he would pay $1 to the pot for each cut. This stopped a lot of nonsense but still allowed the suspicious or superstitious player to cut the cards.

7. Many people enjoy a beer or two, but a serious poker game is no place for heavy drinking. Although drunks may well drop a bundle of cash, they slow down the play and take away much of the pleasure of the game. When they wake up the next morning with a headache

and an empty pocket, they have the feeling (to one degree or another) that you took advantage of them.

8. Post-mortems and rabbit hunting slow down a poker game and should be discouraged. If a rabbit hunter proves himself to be too much of a nuisance in a serious poker group, the players are better off without him. One way to rid the group of such a player is to move (or float) the game and stop inviting him. Another way to improve the situation is to correct his lack of etiquette at the table. But some of these fellows can be so persistent that it seems, at times, as if the only way to rid your game of one is to do to him what Doc Holliday did to Ed Bailey.

Holliday, Bailey and others were playing poker at Ft. Griffin, Texas. Bailey was an especially obstinate rabbit hunter. He even looked at the players' discards and dead hands, often making cutting remarks on how the hand had been played. Now Holliday, like most serious poker players, held that a man had no right to see his hand unless he paid to see it. Several times he strongly advised Bailey to "play poker." But Bailey kept pushing, not only straining poker etiquette and gentlemanly relations, but also stepping over the line and into the realm of cheating at cards. During the showdown hand, Holliday and Bailey were head to head in a pot. Bailey started fingering around in the discards and deadwood, apparently hunting a card that would improve his poker hand. Without a word, Holliday threw in his own hand face down and reached for the pot. Quickly Bailey went for his gun, but Holliday was quicker with his knife, which, as he said, stuck Bailey "just below the brisket!" Exit one rabbit hunter.

Getting rid of some kibitzers is almost as difficult, although I've never known of anybody's having to pull a knife on one. The following recap of a little story from *Playboy* says about all there is to say about kibitzers:

Four men were trying to play poker in the presence of a particularly irritating kibitzer. When the nuisance went out of the room to mix a drink, the players decided to make up a game so that he wouldn't know what was going on and would, hopefully, shut up.

When the kibitzer returned, the players went through the absurdly complicated mechanics of the sham game. Looking at his hand, the dealer announced that he had a "mingle" and bet $1. The second player raised $1 on strength of a "snazzle." The third player folded. After pretending to study the situation at length, the fourth player announced that he held a "farfle" and raised $2.

"You're crazy," barked the kibitzer. "You're never going to beat a mingle and a snazzle with a lousy farfle!"

9. The privilege of dealer's choice is much abused in the typical Friday night group. Some of these sessions are quite way out, and the dealer may invent his own game or variation. The trouble with sessions of this sort is that too much time is spent explaining the mechanics of chimerical games, settling disputes over one point or another with impromptu rulings, and grumbling, "That's not the way we played Razzle back in Yeehaw Junction!" I've even seen some dullards who waste a lot of time in trying to decide on what to deal.

Because of all the confusion, sensible groups settle on a dozen or so games and stick pretty much to one variation of each. Seven-Card Stud High-Low, for example, is played by three scales and three methods of declaration. If the game were not standardized within the group, each dealer would have to specify exactly which variation he intended to deal. His announcement would be something like: "Seven-Card Stud High-Low Split. Wheel is your best low hand. Straights and flushes can swing. Last bettor, last raiser, or high man has to declare first. Swingers have to win both ways to win either way." Then he would probably have to repeat all this at least once for the benefit of those players who were holding a post-mortem on how the previous hand should have been played. But if the group agrees to one variation, the dealer can shorten the name to "Seven High-Low" and everybody will know what he means. Some groups agree on a variation that will be understood *unless the dealer calls otherwise.* For example, California Lowball will be understood unless the dealer specifies either the sixty-four or the seventy-five scales.

10. Have a firm understanding on betting limits and conduct the game accordingly. Peeking at another man's hole card, for example, may be permitted in some penny ante sessions, but it's quite another matter in high stakes. The betting limits influence not only the conduct of the game but also higher poker strategy and the principles of winning play. The bluff, for example, may be a powerful tactic in high stakes but only a playful gesture in penny ante.

Here are some of the more popular methods of limiting the betting:

Table Stakes. One way to fix the limit in big-money poker is to play table stakes, in which no player may bet more than the amount of cash, or number of chips, that he has on the table at the moment. A player may add to his stack from time to time between deals, but never during the course of a hand. In other words, he can't wait until he catches a lock before pulling out a bankroll. Nor can he take money off the table during a hand. Usually, a minimum takeout is required in table stakes.

In some circles, ratholing is not permitted, but is common practice among the winners in other circles. If ratholing is accepted in your group, it is usually wise to pocket your original takeout after you get well ahead in the session; then you have that comfortable feeling that you are playing with the other fellow's money.

Table stakes is sometimes played in conjunction with pot limit. In other words, you can bet the size of the pot if you have that much on the table.

A tap bet is not uncommon in table stakes, and such a bet often creates side pots. For example, player A taps for $200. Player B has only $50 in front of him, so he "goes all in" for that amount. Player C has $150, and also goes all in. Player D has more than $200 and calls the bet in full. Thus, three pots are formed. The main pot contains all the money put in up until the tap, in addition to $50 from all four players (the amount of B's table stake). This leaves $150 of A's bet that B could not call, so a side pot is made and it cannot be won by player B. But Player C could call only $150 of A's tap, so the side pot will contain $100 each from players A, C, and D. Then a second side pot will contain $50 each from players A and D. Either A or D can win all three pots; C can win both the main pot and the first side pot; and B can win only the main pot. If B does win the main pot, players A, C, and D contest for the first side pot. If C wins it, players A and D compete for the second side pot.

When a player folds, he has no further interest in either the main pot or the side pots.

Pot Limit. As indicated above, this popular limit system is exactly the way its name sounds: The maximum bet permissible at any particular time is the size of the pot at the moment. The only point of confusion arises when a player raises. An example will clear this up.

Say the pot contains $10. Player A bets the pot, which now grows to $20. Player B wants to raise the maximum amount. First he calls player A's bet, which puts a total of $30 into the pot (the original $10 plus A's bet plus B's call). This is the maximum amount that B can raise. After B raises $30, player C can call and then raise $90.

Some groups play half-pot limit, which makes a mighty good session. Others combine pot limit with table stakes.

A few groups also play pot limit with a ceiling or maximum bet. With a ceiling of $50, for example, any player can bet or raise the size of the pot up to, but not more than, $50. Having a ceiling is a wise curb in social groups where players are permitted to put checks into the pot, pull shy, and so on. Without such a ceiling or a table stake limitation, someone, sooner or later, will get in over his head.

Bet the Raise. In this limit system, a player may bet as much as was previously put into the pot at one time. For example, player A bets $2. Player B may raise $2 by putting $4 into the pot (the call plus the raise). Player C may raise $4 by putting $8 into the pot (the $4 call plus the $4 raise). Player D may raise $8, and so on.

Fixed Limit Poker. By far the most popular method of limiting what's at stake in a poker session is to fix a minimum and maximum bet, where the minimum bet is usually the same as the ante. Some of the more common limits are nickle and quarter; quarter and a dollar; half and two; one and ten; and so on. Some groups, especially where draw poker is popular, have three limits; in 10-20-30, for example, the minimum bet is ten units, the maximum bet before the draw is 20 units, and the maximum bet after the draw is 30 units.

In my opinion, a maximum limit of $10 or $20 with an ante of $1 per player is a much more expensive game than pot limit or table stakes with a 25¢ ante. I want to emphasize also that the limit alone is not necessarily indicative of how expensive a particular poker session is. I once sat in on a loose game in Tennessee. There were 12 players. The limit was $5 with a maximum of three raises. They called the game Banana, but it was only an expensive variation of Omaha. The first betting interval followed the first down card, thus making for a total of seven betting intervals.

On the very first hand I played, the man under the gun bet $5. There were three raises before it was my turn to act. I held a queen and finally called (because the raising and calling seemed to indicate that the other players had each other's aces and kings!). On the next down card, I caught another queen and again there were three raises in front of me and again I called a total of $20. The first widow card was also a lady, and of course I was raring to go then. At the showdown, my triplets were beaten in two places. One guy made a flush, and another hit a runt straight! My losses on that one hand were well over $100. After playing in two more sessions with that Banana bunch, I decided that it was too expensive (and too much of a gamble) for my blood—although I continued playing in a regular pot limit session with a ceiling bet of $50, as well as occasionally sitting on a table stakes house game!

Poverty Poker. If you play a sorry game of poker and have trouble limiting your losses to what you can afford, try Poverty Poker. Here's a description from George Coffin's *Fortune Poker*:

"Recently we heard of a stop loss gadget used by a close group of friends who met weekly. Their game is 25¢ limit with $30 free wheeling. After losing $30, the maximum loss permitted for one evening, a player continues to get cards and he calls all bets and raises without putting any chips or money in the pot! Until he wins a pot, he plays free!

"In another and probably fairer type of Poverty Poker, a bankrupt player is 'loaned' one stack by the bank.

"If he loses it all, he must quit but pays nothing; or if he is short when the game ends, he pays back what chips he has left. In either case the winners pay his loss when the game ends.

"He collects no cash from the bank until he has repaid all his 'borrowed' chips."

In still another form of Poverty Poker, you assign a value to the chips of five times what you paid for them. In other words, you are gambling only 20¢ on the dollar. I've never noticed a name in print for such a poker session, but novelist John D. MacDonald, who writes the Travis McGee books, told me that in Philadelphia they used to call it Pussycat Poker. It's a fitting name.

11. Have a firm understanding within the group about what beats what. Although a single, universal scale for lowball and high-low poker hasn't yet fully evolved, the rank of regular poker hands has

been established. Almost everyone knows that a flush beats a straight all over the world, but if in doubt see "Rank of Poker Hands" in the Glossary and Table I in Part Two.

Currently, many nonstandard hands are recognized from group to group, and the more common ones are listed under "Special Hands" in Part Three. Whether all or any of these hands will one day become widely accepted as standard poker remains to be seen. Players who object to admitting Dutch Straights and Big Dogs into the rank of poker hands should remember that straights and flushes were, not too long ago, nonstandard poker hands that brought much protest from diehards! The straight first gained one of the Hoyle books in 1875, and it ranked above two pairs but below triplets! As late as 1937, however, another Hoyle book said that straights were not allowed in stud poker!

Anyhow, it's best to have an understanding about low scales and special hands—lest you find yourself bucking a mingle and a snazzle with a lousy farfle!

2.

Managing Your Money

Serious poker cannot be played without money. Unless cash or something of monetary value backs up the chips, such principles of poker as the bluff lack force. Some philosophical gamblers—Nick the Greek, for one—have said that money should be important only as a means of keeping score. Even so, the score in poker is reckoned not by a tally of the pots a player has won during a session but by the amount of capital he has gained or lost.

The importance of money management becomes apparent when you consider that it's possible to lose dozens of hands and still come out ahead when you finally do win one. In poker, you can come out ahead over the long haul even if, by some quirk of probability, you do not catch your fair share of good cards. Such a victory over chance is possible because you don't have to spend your capital, other than a small ante, on poker hands that do not figure to win.

Without question, *conserve your capital during play* is the most important rule in money management. The steadfast winner doesn't piddle away his chips on sorry hands. He refuses the temptation to "see one more card," as the saying goes in poker games across the land. He doesn't "call because it's cheap" unless he has the odds in his favor. I know one player who often makes a few loose calls during the early rounds of betting because, as he puts it, "I need a project." Sure, a few chips tossed in while it's cheap to play don't seem like much at the time; but over the hours they determine whether you go home winner or loser, and over the years they add up to a considerable pile of cash.

Another important rule in money management is *conserve your capital after the poker session is over*. Far too many poker players squander their winnings. Easy come, easy go. If they win $500, they feel free to buy that new sofa for the wife; if they lose $500 during the next session, they may well find themselves sleeping on it for the next few nights. So, whenever you have a good run of cards, remember that they will cool off sooner or later.

Wise players keep a poker kitty—preferably a separate bank account—and operate on a sound money management basis. A good rule of thumb is to lose no more than 5 percent of your poker capital at any one session. Most players aren't going to have that much capital to tie up for poker, so 10 or even 20 percent is a reasonable figure. Take 10 percent for the purpose of illustration. If you have a playing capital of $1000, you can lose no more than $100 in one poker session. If you do lose the $100 stake, your total poker capital is reduced to $900; therefore, you could lose no more than $90 during the next session. But if you *win* $140 during the next session, your capital has mounted to $1040. Assuming that $1000 is enough capital for your game (which of course depends on the betting limits and pace), then you have a $40 surplus. Feel free to spend this $40 in any way you see fit, but it is best to work toward some worthwhile goal.

It would be possible for a player to stick to the 10 percent rule until he lost so much of his capital that he would not have an adequate stake for his game. In this case, he is probably bucking superior players and should find another game with lower limits and poorer players. If the lower limit action doesn't appeal to him, he should nevertheless stick with it until he builds up his capital and improves his skill enough to take on the big boys again.

What is an adequate stake? In limit poker with a reasonable ante, I would say from 25 to 50 times the maximum bet. Thus, in a $2 limit game, from $50 to $100 should last a competent player long enough to see how the cards are running. The higher stake would be required in razzle-dazzle games like Cincinnati Liz or Bedsprings; the smaller stake, in conservative games like Jacks or Five-Card Stud.

An adequate stake is especially important in a limit game where one plans to play the percentages for hour after hour. It's my opinion, however, that the short money player has the advantage in table stakes or pot limit action. First, the short money player has a mathematical advantage in the big pots, simply because he can "go all in" during the early rounds of betting, thereby getting good odds on his money before the high-rollers bet each other out. Second, his losses are limited to what he can afford. To be sure, a short money player is more likely to go broke in a particular session than a moneybags player. He will lose often. But when he does win, he can win very big indeed in relation to what he stands to lose.

I knew a player who would never take more than $100 (the minimum take-out) to a table stakes game. If he lost his stake, even on the first hand, he would go home. He might lose several times in a row. But when he did win, he would make up for his previous losses. Even following a big win, he would bring only $100 to the next game. Niggardly? Yes. But it was a "house" game run by professional gamblers, not a social gathering. As he told me, "It's the only way to play high-stakes poker—unless you're a rich man." I think he's right, except that an inadequate stake doesn't give the expert full room for strategy unless he gets lucky enough to win a few good pots at the outset.

Most gamblers will disagree violently with what I have said about the short money player having a mathematical edge, and they have support from some scholars. John Maynard Keynes, for one, said in his *A Treatise on Probability* that the gambler (in poker as well as on the stock exchange) is in a bad position if his capital is smaller than his opponent's. Keynes concluded that poor men should not gamble and that millionaires should do nothing else. There is, of course, much truth in what Keynes said. Still, I'll play pot limit poker with any millionaire if he'll put up $1,000,000 against my $100. If I did play with a millionaire, however, I would certainly have to put a ceiling on my losses. If I didn't, I could easily be wiped out financially.

The comments made above are extreme examples of another important rule of money management: Limit your losses but not your winnings. For several reasons. First, you stand to win a good deal of money at small risk. (The player who quits when he gets a little ahead, but who plunges deeper and deeper when he starts losing, follows the opposite advice and stands to win little at great risk.) Second, most of us—but not quite all—play better when we are winning than when we are losing. Our perceptions are better. We feel better. Third, and perhaps most important, you will never let poker ruin you financially if you follow this rule.

♥ ♥ ♥

Other aspects of money management have to do with sizing your bets. In many instances it is better to have one player call a $20 bet than to have two players call a $10 bet, or four players call a $5 bet. If you're betting on the come—say on a fourflush in Jacks—it's far better to have four players at $5 each, so that the odds will be about right; but if you've already got a pretty strong hand made—say three aces—it's far better to have one player at $20, so that you won't have so many players trying to fill straights and flushes on you.

The importance of sizing your bets may be illustrated by a simple example. Players A and B are butting heads in a hand of lowball. Player A makes a wheel and bets $10. Player B makes a seventy-six and calls. Now reverse the situation on the next deal. Player B makes the wheel and bets $20. Player A makes the seventy-six and calls. Clearly, player B is $10 ahead on the exchange. In real poker, however, the situation is much more complex. If in the latter case player B had bet $50, he would be $40 ahead *provided that* player A called. If A didn't call the $50 bet, B would be $10 behind on the two hands. Which would be the better bet depends a good deal on the character of the two players involved. Note also that player A might call a $50 bet made by player B—but might not call the same bet made by player C!

The sizing of bets is fairly cut and dried in low-limit poker. The better players will usually make the maximum bet whenever they believe they hold the winning hands. In table stakes, however, the maximum bet is limited only by how much money the players have in front of them at the moment. Still, the size of the pot is a good index for the higher bets.

By the way, how much money a player has already put into a pot often causes gross violations of sound betting principles. It is, of course, unfortunate if a particular player has a lot of money "invested" in a pot; but only the size of the pot at the moment, not how much he personally has put into it earlier in the hand, should determine whether he calls a particular bet. In other words, a player shouldn't send good money after bad. Yet, the saying "I've got too much in-vested to quit now" will always be heard in poker games.

♥ ♥ ♥

Another important consideration in money management is the size of the ante. Very tight players are better off with no ante at all; loose players, with a large ante. If one plays too tight in a high-ante game, he is sure to lose. If one plays too loose in a small-ante game, he is sure to lose. Therefore, the complete poker player must vary his style somewhat according to the size of the ante. Generally, the lower the ante in fixed-limit games, the more certain the expert is to come out ahead; the higher the ante, the more he must gamble.

In limit poker, I prefer an ante of about 10 percent of the maxi-mum bet, and certainly no more than 25 percent. Thus, in a $2 limit game, the ante should be about 25¢ per player, and no more than 50¢

It's much more difficult to set the ante for pot limit or table stakes. My own preference is to base the ante (if I have any say-so in the matter) not on the size of the bets but on my stake or on how much I am willing to lose in the game. If I went into a table stakes game with only $50, I certainly wouldn't want to ante more than $1 per player.

The ante has been called a player's "overhead." The term is fairly accurate except that the overhead is returned to a player whenever he wins a pot. There is another form of overhead that the player seldom gets back. In casino or house games, money is extracted from the players in one way or another. Some housemen take as much as 5 per-cent of each pot. Five percent is much too high, and no honest player can come out ahead over the long haul under such a rake-off. The house will get all the money.

Some housemen drag a quarter or a half dollar out of each pot. This is sometimes reasonable enough, depending upon the limits of betting and the size of the pots. But many such pot-cutters have sticky fingers, and I have seen a few who could cut a single pot four or five times so inconspicuously that the players didn't seem to notice it. I dislike this sort of chipping even more than I dislike the 5 percent fee. (At least with 5 percent you know what you're up against!)

I think a standard hourly fee is by far the best way for the house to get its cut. A buck and a half per hour per player is reasonable enough, at least from the player's viewpoint. On the other hand, a really good house game might have a high overhead, since the houseman must sometimes pay off the fuzz, provide protection against hold-up men, and keep cardsharpers out of the game. If a house doesn't provide this protection, then the players are leaving themselves wide open on all three counts. Why pay to play there if such protection isn't provided?

I really prefer to play in a private game, where the players chip out enough to pay for the cards, snacks, and hotel room. If the game is in a private residence, I like for the host to chip out enough for his wife to pay a maid to clean the place up the next day.

♥ ♥ ♥

Poker took on a new importance a few years ago when it was used as a model "money management" game for the study of capitalism in *Theory of Games and Economic Behavior* by John von Neumann and Oskar Morganstern, both of Princeton's Institute for Advanced Studies and both of A-bomb fame. Part of their theory—vastly over-simplified—is that if you put more chips (free) into a poker game, you have inflation; withdraw chips, and you have deflation. Wild cards have the same effect. I am certain that tight players (bears) tend to induce deflation and loose players (bulls) tend to induce inflation. I am also certain that some master poker players control the pace of a session by "shooting it up" when they are winning or by "getting behind the log" when they are losing. This ability may well be the ultimate in money management!

3.

Bluffing

Ask a poker buff to tell his favorite yarn, and I'll lay even-money odds that a bluff will be involved. Sneak the word "poker" into one of those spontaneous word-association tests that psychologists administer, and I'll give 2-to-1 odds that the answer will be either "bluff" or its mask, "poker face." Plop a big stack of money into the pot during a hand of Five-Card Stud, and I'll lay 10-to-1 odds that the question behind the opponent's wrinkled brow will be: "Is he bluffing?"

Nor is the bluff limited to poker. Threaten the boss with an ultimatum for a raise, tell the ladylove that it's now or never, dare the bully to put up or shut up—in life, as in poker, you bluff at your peril or to your gain. Although the bluff would no doubt exist independently of poker and its predecessors (ancient Persian *as nas*, English bragg, and French *ambigu* all embodied the bluff), it is nonetheless the most adventurous idea ever perpetuated by a card game. Owing largely to the bluff, poker has influenced our thinking on life, love, business, and even war. In fact, the mathematical theory of games, mentioned at the end of the last chapter, was given a high security classification by the armed services during World War II!

In a popular treatment of the highly technical theory, John McDonald called the bluff the *spirit* of poker. The statement is valid within the context of poker as a game. Bluffing, a spunky player can win the pot without having the best hand. This possibility of individual character and cunning and even foolhardiness winning out, by bluffing, and in spite of the run of the cards, distinguishes poker from such pure gambling games as craps and roulette.

If, on the other hand, poker were to be divested of the bluff—if all players had to size their bets in strict relation to the hierarchic value of their hands, which in turn is based on mathematical probability—poker would be reduced to mere chance. It would require less skill, less sense of strategy, less faculty for judgment. Other than knowing the correct odds against making a successful draw to a bobtail straight (and similar carding situations), the knowledgeable player would have only a negligible advantage over the tyro and the dullard. Except for patience, individual character traits would not be important. A computer would play a perfect game. In short, poker without the bluff would indeed have no spirit. It would quickly die out. No—it wouldn't have become the great American card game in the first place.

Spirit or not, however, the bluff, as such, is generally a losing proposition. The player who bluffs every hand will surely go broke. The image of the expert player as frequent bluffer is false, and the famed poker face is largely a myth. Steady winners do not bluff often. Yet, bluff they must, from time to time. Moreover, they must be *caught* bluffing for the purpose of strategy over a long series of plays. In other words, the poker player has to bluff occasionally to keep his opponents guessing. Such is the nature of the game.

How often should the complete strategist run a bluff in poker? One authority recommends that he bluff until he is caught twice in a particular session. Well, twice is a good enough rule of thumb—but what happens in a regular game after the opposition takes note of the "twice" habit? To be effective strategically, the bluff must be completely random—but yet not spontaneous, and not whenever a certain situation takes shape. Far too many players, for instance, have an urge to bluff on a busted flush, so that a one-card draw does not leave their bluff on random footing.

Can the expert player show an outright profit on the bluff? Perhaps. If he really is an expert. Paradoxically, he can make more successful bluffs against competent players than against poor ones. A poker adage: Never bluff a poor player, a heavy winner, or a heavy loser. There is a good deal of truth in the statement; but the expert, who expects to turn a profit on his bluffs in addition to strategical value, will not always follow any such advice. Some few players are relatively easy to bluff when they are heavy winners or heavy losers, and a smattering of poor players are easy to bluff. It depends on the man, and on the situation at each particular bluffing instance, and on the limits of the game, and on the general disposition of the group.

Another paradox is that the expert can make more successful bluffs from a poor betting position than from a good one. For example, player A opens in Jacks with two small pairs. Player B calls, holding four cards to a flush. Player C calls with a pair of aces. After the draw, player A checks to the possible flush. Having busted the flush, player B also checks. Knowing that the flush (or straight) hasn't connected, player C bets, hoping to bluff A out. Most likely player A will call, simply because C was in a "good" bluffing position. The bluff would have been more likely to succeed if B and C had changed seats: Player A checks, C bets *into* the possible flush, thereby indicating strength.

The squeeze play works even better. Let C open with a pair of jacks. Player A calls with a pair of kings. Player B calls with a fourflush. None of them improves on the draw. Bluffing, C bets the limit. He knows that A (if A is a competent player) has a pair higher than jacks. He also knows that B drew one card to a flush or straight because he (B) would have raised on two pairs or a triplet-kicker hand. Chances are that B missed the flush. Thus, by betting under the gun, which would on first thought seem to be a very bad bluffing position, C puts A in the whipsaw, and his bluff is likely to succeed. Of course, B may connect on the flush— but, then, the bluff is a hazardous play under any circumstances.

♥ ♥ ♥

The big payoff on the bluff comes indirectly, and more or less perversely, not from the mentalities of game theory and strategy, but from a deeper realm of the gambler's psyche. The expert profits on the bluff in an inverse way, at the expense of the poor player and the psychologically chronic loser. How? Why? Because the poor player, and especially the chronic loser, suspects almost every bet of being a bluff. The mere possibility of a bluff gives him the excuse he needs to get into the action, to give his money away.

Of course, the poor player loses in a number of other ways, such as drawing to a short pair at unfavorable odds. The chronic loser, however, may be, in other respects, a competent poker player. He may know the correct odds and may even have enough self-control and patience to play accordingly. In fact, the correct mathematical odds may even support his rationalization of calling a suspected bluff.

I used to play poker with a professional mathematician. He knew how to figure the odds, and he played by them. Yet he seldom won. His downfall was not that he bluffed too often or that he bucked the odds by drawing to inside straights, but simply that he called too many end bets. One night we were playing a seven-handed game of draw poker. Dollar ante; $50 maximum bet. He opened for $5 with a pair of kings. Another player called. I called with an ace-high fourflush. Of course I knew that the odds were against my filling the flush; on the other hand, I knew that if I did fill it the mathematician would more than likely call my $50 end bet. Luckily, I squeezed out an all-red hand of hearts. The mathematician caught another pair to go with his kings, so he bet $20 after the draw. The middle played folded. I called and raised $50. He called. I showed him my flush and raked in the pot. He shook his head contemptuously, saying, "The odds against making that flush were 4¼ to 1!"

No doubt he thought I had made a bad play by drawing to the flush in the first place. Perhaps I had. (But I would not have made the draw against any other player at the table, because I knew that they might not call my end bet if I did connect on the flush.) I think *he* made a very bad play by calling my $50 raise. True, the mathematical odds had been 4¼ to 1. But I probably don't bluff more than once in a hundred hands, which put the empirical odds at 99 to 1 that I wasn't bluffing! What's more, I wouldn't make an outright bluff against that particular player once in a thousand hands of draw poker, which put the odds at 999 to 1 that I wasn't bluffing!

With other chronic losers it's not the mathematics that provides the excuse to suspect a bluff; rather, it's a point of honor with them to "keep you honest," as the saying goes. They hold it nothing short of dishonor to be bluffed out when they actually held the winning hand. In a way they are right. But good players

—consistent winners—have no such scruples about throwing in a winning hand; if they suffer from breach of code, they do so on the way to the bank to deposit the money they have won from the chivalrous. In short, the player who never throws in a winning hand is a sure loser. (But the complete strategist must make an unsound call from time to time, for the same reason that he must bluff from time to time.)

Another kind of steady loser seems to harbor some sort of persecution complex. He thinks people are trying to push him around all the time, that the other players are trying to bully him out of pots. I knew one such player, and he attributed his heavy poker losses to bad luck. "Oh, you catch your share of winning cards," I said, feeling sorry for the guy and sincerely wanting to give him some helpful advice. "The trouble is that you call too many big bets on mediocre hands." He bowed up at me, saying, "I know you guys are trying to run me out of those big pots!"

Still another kind of loser is the one who *does* bluff too often. Perhaps bluffing and throwing his money around make him feel important, or else he is simply foolhardy. A few steady players lapse into this category when they have been drinking, when they are losing beyond their means, or when a woman is present. Anyway, I believe it is far better to be a chronic bluffer than a chronic caller. Another old poker adage sums the matter up pretty well: A fool bets on anything—but only a sucker calls on nothing.

♥ ♥ ♥

A fellow once told me, in no uncertain terms, that I am full of bull when it comes to bluffing in lowball draw. "Bluffing per se can be very profitable in many lowball situations," he said. "The classic case is when you and your opponent draw one card each. The odds are about 1½ to 1 [actually 27 to 20] that your opponent will not make a 9 or better; therefore, you have a bet in the blind, regardless of what you catch! Percentagewise, this bluff will pay off, and it should always be made whenever your opponent draws one or more cards."

He made a good point. But, frankly, I doubt that his bluffing attempts are all that successful, simply because I doubt that he bluffs as often as he thinks he does! What he described was a percentage bet, not an outright bluff. An example will show the difference:

Both you and your opponent draw one card each. You catch a jack, which of course is a pretty sorry lowball hand. You bet. He folds. But have you really bluffed him? He could have caught a king, a queen, or a spike card. There are four kings, four queens, and twelve cards that would pair him; therefore the chances are about 20 in 47 that you have him beaten with your jack. This means that if you make the bet 47 times, there will be about 20 times that your jack will win in case there is a showdown. In these 20 cases, you have nothing to gain by betting (except perhaps to mix up your play and possibly to keep him from betting *you* out of the pot). So, you see that such a bet is not necessarily a bluff.

If, on the other hand, you paired 8's and bet into your opponent, you would probably be making a real bluff, since it isn't probable that he will pair a card higher than an 8. In this case you have a good deal to gain by betting, because you will lose in a showdown situation.

I recommend betting out on your good hands and occasionally on the sorry hands. The mediocre hands, like 10-low should, I think, be checked after the draw. If your opponent can beat a 10, he'll probably call. If he can't beat it, you would win anyhow in the showdown. If he makes a 7 or better, he'll raise you out of your seat. So why bet a rough 9 or 10 into him?

Actually, betting in lowball shouldn't be discussed independently of position (the topic of Chapter 5). Before leaving lowball bluffery, however, I want to concede that the first bettor has a precarious edge against a single opponent if he always makes the percentage bet whenever both players draw. Until the opposition catches on. Remember that if you *always* have a percentage bet in the blind, then your opponent has a percentage raise!

♥ ♥ ♥

To bluff with intentions, not of winning the pot, but of getting caught is called "advertising." Such a bluff is purely strategic, it is geared to lose on the hand in question, but to pay off on a series of plays in the future. During the past few years, Albert H. Morehead and others have taken the concept to task. They agree that the bluff has advertising value, but they maintain that a player should bluff to win, not to be caught. Don't worry, they say, you'll be caught often enough.

Well, I agree that one should bluff to win; otherwise, it's not really a bluff. Yet, the advertising concept deserves serious thought, and, in some bluffing occasions, it might well be better to be caught, depending on how much potential advertising value the hand in question holds. The success of all advertising depends on its reaching a large audience with sufficient impact. Consequently, it is best to bluff or be caught bluffing when there are eight players at the table (but not necessarily active in the pot) than when there are only three. And it is by far best to advertise on an unusual hand, one that will be remembered, rather than on an ordinary busted flush. If, for example, player A bluffs on a 10-high in lowball, his bluff will not cause a lot of comment at the table and will not stick long in the minds of his opponents. On the other hand, if he happened to catch four natural 10's in lowball, played them pat, and bet them to the hilt, then it would, I think, be best to be caught, simply because it would be a bluff that his opponents would long remember!

To bluff too often, however, with intentions of getting caught really undermines the nature of the bluff. The very idea saps the "spirit" of poker.

There is an old poker tale about a man who obviously bluffed to win, not to advertise. Returning from the gold fields, the forty-niners were rounding Cape Horn by schooner. The game was Straight Draw, no limit. The units of betting were little bags of gold. They were playing topside, and the wind occasionally blew a card face up. Finally, they made a rule that a card so exposed during the deal or draw could be retained or replaced, at the recipient's option. While the hero was playing for a big pot, his one-card draw blew over. He grabbed for it. The wind blew it along the deck. He chased it. The card went overboard and into the choppy water. Without hesitation, he jumped in after it. When the schooner had been brought about and the hero hoisted aboard, he put the wet card—the five of diamonds—onto his poker hand. Then he bet all his bags of gold. Of course no one called the huge bet; quite obviously, the five of diamonds had filled a straight flush or something. After the hero had raked in the pot and had gone to change his wet clothes, someone turned over his cards to see what sort of powerhouse he had held. To their surprise, there were four spades along with the five of diamonds! Now *that* is spunk and spirit.

A close examination of the literature of poker, including the lore and the tall tales, would probably confirm that the bluff is indeed the spirit of the game. It is certainly the most popular aspect of poker, as Hollywood script writers, TV writers, and advertising specialists know. Still, the consistent winner, unless he is willing to jump overboard, will put more faith in a pair of wired aces than in spiritual matters.

4.

Analyzing Your Opponents

At the outset of Chapter 2, I said that serious poker cannot be played without money at stake. I know of but a single exception. One night I visited a friend of mine, who had built himself a house atop a mountain, to ask whether he would mind sitting in on a poker game while a magazine photographer took some pictures to illustrate an article I had written. My friend didn't take too much to the notion, but his wife and daughter thought it was groovy. Because I got the best of him on that count, I was a bit ahead of the game when we started playing some fun poker a few minutes later. This was around 10 P.M.

At 3 A.M. we were still sitting at the kitchen table knocking heads for a big pile of valueless chips. His wife had gone to bed at midnight, at which time I myself got up to leave. I had to drive about 30 miles and was ready to get off that mountain. But my friend wanted to play. I sat down again—but only on condition that we increase the betting to pot limit.

At about 12:30 his daughter went broke, yawned, and quit the game. I stood to go, wanting to get off the mountain before the roads iced over. My friend would have none of it. He wanted to play poker. We argued. Finally, I sat down again—but only on condition that we increase the betting to table stakes. By then it had become clear to me that I would have to win all his chips or else lose all mine before I could go peaceably.

Luck was with me. Before long I tapped on a sixty-five in Lowball Draw and he called on a slick seven. Immediately he put in to borrow some chips. I refused the loan, saying that there wasn't much point in my winning the chips if I had to give them back to him. We had each given the girls some chips from time to time, he said. That was different, I said.

"They're my chips," he said. "I *own* the goddam chips."

"Then the game is over," I said, standing to go.

"Sit down!" he shouted. Then he jumped up and started searching in drawers and cubbyholes for odd chips. He found a few and played them very tight. I got them one by one, grumbling all the while that I had to risk my big pile against his lone and meager stack.

"Have you got any more?" I asked.

Without a word he got up and searched the house. At length he found a whole boxful of tiny toy chips, about the size of a dime. Now, he said, he had enough to play good poker and would beat me.

"We'll see," I said.

On his deal, I wired 10's back-to-back in Five-Card Stud. But he had an ace up and made a sizable bet. I called.

On the next up card, I caught an 8 and he caught a 9. Quickly he put the deck down and looked at his hole card. That move told me a lot. I knew that he didn't have another ace in the hole, simply because he wouldn't have forgotten his hole card if it had been an ace. He probably held either a 9 or an 8 down; *something* had prompted him to recheck his hole card, and I felt that it was either the 8 I caught or the 9 he caught.

He bet. I raised. He called. I felt even more confident now that he did hold 9's and not aces. He wouldn't have called without a pair, but would have re-raised on aces. I was almost certain that he would have raised on aces because not once over the past several hours had he sandbagged me.

He dealt. I caught a trey. He caught one of my 10's, which may have led him to put me on 8's, not 10's.

He bet rather heavily.

I tapped, pushing out my whole pile of chips.

"How much did you bet?" he asked.

"More than you can call," I said.

"Count your bet," he said.

"You count it," I said. "Look, if you call I win everything. So just push out your chips."

"I could have aces."

"If you do, we'll count the bet." If he had aces, he wouldn't be stalling, I thought.

"I can beat 8's," he said.

"Not if you don't call my tap," I said, glancing at my watch. It was a few minutes past three.

"I'm going to call you," he said. He pushed out his chips.

"My 10's beat your 9's," I said, flipping my hole card and reaching for the pot.

"You're a lucky bastard," he said.

"It's not *all* luck," I said, looking at him over my pile of chips.

He looked me square in the eye. "You're not only a lucky bastard. You're also an arrogant son-of-a-bitch!"

♥ ♥ ♥

Some players are easy to read; others aren't. Some are deceptive; others aren't. Some follow fixed patterns of play; others don't. Obviously, you profit by knowing your opponent, and learning more and more about him from hour to hour, Friday night to Friday night, and year to year not only makes you a better poker player but also puts you wiser to the ways of man.

If you make an effort to become a better observer, you will not often be bored at a poker table. Even when you are not active in a pot, you can use your time advantageously by studying your opponents' habits and mannerisms and voice tones and patterns of play. Keeping a notebook will improve your ability to observe and remember your opponent's behavior. (As Francis Bacon put it, "If a man write little, he had need have a great memory.") How many patterns and habits you can detect is limited only by your eye for detail and how disciplined you are at observing. As a starter, I've listed below a dozen or so observations to indicate the sort of thing to look for. Remember, however, that some poker players seem to be competing for Best Actor awards!

1. When holding strong hands, many poker players are quite eager to get the action started. Often they will say something like "Whose bet is it?" or "It's on you, Joe."

2. When they intend to call or raise, some players will pick up their money or chips before it is their turn to act on their hands. Others will fake this mannerism, hoping to get by on a check.

3. As the story in the first part of this chapter showed, it is usually significant when your opponent checks his hole card in stud forms.

4. How a player stands in a particular session has a bearing, to one degree or another, on how he plays. When winning, some players tighten up considerably to conserve their profit; others take more chances and bluff more often. When losing, some players tighten up because "the cards aren't running" their way; others become desperate and wild and full of bluff, especially if the session is about to break up.

5. Generally, a tight player keeps his chips or money neatly stacked; a sloppy table stake, on the other hand, may indicate a loose player.

6. Some players are reluctant to break large bills. If you want such a player to call your bet, make it easy for him; if you want him to fold, size your bet so that he'll have to break a bill. For example, you're playing $5 limit. Your opponent has a $20 bill and three singles. Bet $3 if you want him to call. Bet $4 if you want him to quit the pot. If he has a good hand, he'll call anyway. But on a borderline call, having to break the bill just might be the straw that broke the camel's back.

7. If drawing light is permitted in your group, don't, as a rule, try to bluff a player who is already shy. He'll have more of a tendency to call than a player who is not already shy in the pot.

8. A glance to the left may indicate that a player is thinking about raising. He has a tendency to glance left to see how many players are behind him, whether they have picked up their money, and so on.

9. When drawing one card to a fourflush, to a bobtail straight, or to two pairs, some players will "sweat them out" and will often jerk or groan or make some other sign when he sees the stranger. Individuals react different ways, and some resort to trickery on this point. So, watch your man over a series of plays.

10. As Irwin Steig pointed out in *Poker for Fun and Profit*, it is difficult to bluff a woman in a poker game because she always wants to know how a plot will unfold. I'm sure there are exceptions, but I think Steig might have something. One nice thing about this point is that it doesn't usually take much observation to tell that your opponent is a woman!

11. When a player starts asking how many cards the other players drew in Jacks and similar games, he's often connected with triplets, or otherwise improved a pair, and wants to know how many opponents were drawing to fourflushes and bobtails. A good observer won't have to ask; he'll know how many cards each active player took.

12. How some players fit their card into their hand on the draw often indicates what they hold. When they have two pairs, for example, they may always fit the draw card in the middle. When a player is going for a flush, he may put the draw card on top of his hand and then mix them up thoroughly before squeezing the stranger out.

13. In high-low forms of stud, a player will usually be more interested in hands that look as though they are going the same way he is going. So, observe what your opponents are observing!

Listing all the ways in which a player may reveal information about his hand would be impossible. Such a casual act as lighting a cigarette may have significance with one opponent but not with another, so that you have to watch each player individually. But don't spend *all* your time observing and analyzing your opponents' play. Remember that you too tip your hand from time to time.

♥ ♥ ♥

My favorite poker story happened because of a player's mannerism. The game was $2 limit and was held in the back of a poolhall. The tightest player in the group was an old stud man, who wore overalls. I'll call him Runt here because he was so short that he usually sat on a stool instead of a chair. Sometimes when he had a good hand—and sometimes when he was setting up a bluff—he would rear back, hold his head as though he were looking at the ceiling, scratch his chin as if in deep thought, and say in a drawn-out voice, "Well-l-l, I believe I'll have to raise it a little bit."

One night we were engaged in a hand of Five-Card Stud. He caught a king on the last up card. An ace showing around the board checked. The owner of the joint bet $2 on wired jacks. Runt looked at his hole card, reared back, raised his head, and started scratching his chin. The houseman, a good poker player who joked around a lot, knew then that his jacks were beaten, since Runt very seldom made a bluff on an end bet. So, while Runt was scratching his chin, the houseman winked at the rest of us and quickly switched hole cards with him. At length Runt said, "Well-l-l-l, I believe I'll have to raise it a little bit. Four plays."

The rest of us folded around the board to the houseman. "I'll look," he said, tossing in $2. "Hole card?"

"Kings!" Runt said, smiling. He reached down and flipped over a red jack. His mouth popped open. His eyes popped out. He shook his head, as if to clear a blurred vision. The red jack was still there. "Goddamn," he said, "Goddamn, I've been screwed and there ain't a man in the house that I can whup!"

After all the laughter died down, the houseman gave Runt the pot fair and square. From that time on, however, old Runt never looked up at the ceiling when he held a good hand. Instead, he kept his eyes on his hole card!

5.

Playing Position

An old pro once told me that position is the key to strategy. He was speaking of Lowball Draw, a game in which position is especially pertinent. For this reason—and because I agree with the old pro—I have chosen Lowball Draw as the game to illustrate some of the principles of position. Special situations in other forms of poker (such as playing declaratory position in high-low split) are discussed in other chapters or under the "Dealer's Choice" games in Part Three. General situations are schematized in the diagrams at the end of this chapter.

Position in poker is a little hard to define in a few words, but it has to do with the relation of the players to each other. An individual's position at a particular betting instant has to do with the number and type of players who have acted on their hands before him and the others who will have to act on their hands behind him. Even the novice quickly recognizes the disadvantage of being under the gun in Jacks, but his sense of position seldom extends much further. Such a player is a sitting pigeon in a game like Lowball Draw. The competent Lowball player, on the other hand, jockeys for position almost as much as he plays his cards, for he knows that the value of his hand is determined not only by its rank but also by where he sits in relation to the opener and the dealer, as well as to the various types of players.

Often the expert's position will be a deciding influence on whether he checks, bets, calls, raises, or folds on a pat 9; whether he sandbags a slick 6; or whether he bluffs on a bust hand. His position will have a bearing not only on his betting but also on his carding. Moreover, when considered in relation to the betting sequence in a particular deal, his opponent's position is an important key in assessing the probable strength of his hand.

Position in relation to the dealer. Your position in relation to the dealer bears on the betting before the draw and on the carding during the draw. It has no importance after the draw, except as a historical key to playing your hand and assessing your opposition.

Before the draw, the man under the gun is, of course, in the worst possible position because he has to act on his hand first, without any indication of what the players behind him are going to do. Except for making an occasional "unsound" play for strategical purposes, the player under the gun should open in Lowball Draw only when he holds a good pat hand—an 8 or better (based on the California Lowball scale, a reasonable ante, and a full table). Even then he may choose to sandbag, especially if he thinks that opening under the gun will reveal the strength of his hand.

A good drawing hand, such as A-2-3-7-K, should usually be checked under the gun. The odds against making a 7-low are about 3 to 1, and the ante will not, as a rule, offer good odds for a bet of any size. In a loose game with seven or eight players, you would probably get several calls, making the odds right. But you might also get raised. So, why not check, in a loose game, and let one of the others open?

In a tight game for big money, seldom open under the gun on any one-card draw. If you do, you may be raised, the pot might not offer favorable odds, and you will surely be in the worst position again after the draw (unless you plan to hazard a percentage bet). It is true that in a tight game anyone who opens under the gun suggests strength and may win the pot without a contest. But the pot will be small.

Very seldom open under the gun with a pat 9 or 10. What will you do with it after the draw? It's not a betting hand—and you can't check it. To check a pat hand after the draw in a heads-up game is almost like turning a 9 or a 10 face up. Check it *before* the draw (so that you will be in a better position *after* the draw). Then, if anyone opens, either throw your pat 9 in or else raise to drive out as many players as possible and to discourage further betting after the draw.

Whether you throw in the pat 9 or 10, or raise on it, should be influenced one way or the other by what sort of player opened the pot, his betting position, how many calls are made in front of you, and so on. If your patsy is a smooth one, thereby offering the option of a one-card draw, your carding position can become very important, as will be discussed a little later.

These rules of thumb about opening in the worst position—under the gun—can be slackened as your position becomes more favorable. But slacken them very little, especially if you are playing with a bunch of sandbaggers.

Although the dealer enjoys the best position because every other player at the table has to speak before him, this does not alter the odds against making a one-card draw to a 7 and it does not transform a pat ninety-eight into a hand that can be bet with confidence after the draw. Since every player has indicated weakness by checking, the dealer can open on a good one-card draw or a good pat hand. To open on a mediocre pat hand, the dealer should have an option of a good draw. If he opens on a pat 10-9-8-7-2 and gets raised by a sandbagger or runs into another pat hand, what can he do with it? On a 10-6-5-4-A, however, he can either hold pat or draw one card, depending on his opponent's carding.

In short, to open the pot at all puts you in a precarious betting position both before and after the draw. On the other hand, *somebody* has got to open those pots lest the game become very dull. So . . . in a fun game with the boys on Friday night, open more frequently than you would in a blood game—if you want to be invited back.

Before leaving the subject of position in relation to the dealer, its effect on carding must be considered. Generally, the man under the gun is at a disadvantage here because he has to draw first. In Lowball, however, carding is not quite as complicated as in Jacks and similar games where carding gives room for a good deal of deception and strategy, as discussed in Chapter 6. If a man draws one card in Lowball, it means only that he holds four small cards; in Jacks, he could be drawing to a straight, a flush, four-of-a-kind, triplets, two pairs, or even one pair. In Lowball, carding options become important only when you hold a relatively mediocre pat hand, to which you may want to draw if you run into trouble.

When two pat hands tangle in Lowball, however, carding position in relation to the dealer can be very important, as indicated above. If you hold a mediocre pat hand, you will want to be the last to draw so that you will know whether another pat hand is out, in which case you may choose to draw. If, on the other hand, you suspect your opponent of also holding a mediocre pat hand, but one which probably has you beaten, a bit of bluffery might be in order if you are in an otherwise *unfavorable* carding position. The trick here is to raise before the draw to indicate strength and then to hold pat in front of your opponent. If you have assessed his holding correctly, he will probably come off his patsy and draw, thereby giving you a definite advantage.

Carding in Lowball Draw, then, is usually limited to pat hands of dubious value but which offer the option of a draw. Even here your carding position will be subordinate, usually, to your betting position. Besides, you can't jockey for carding position because you can't check the draw!

Position in relation to the opener. The ideal calling position is immediately to the opener's right, because in that position you will be the last to call the bet and will know exactly what odds the pot offers and will know further that the bet will not be raised behind you. Also, you will be in good position after the draw.

Your worst calling position is when the man on your right opens, because the bet is apt to be raised after you call and because you do not know what odds the pot will offer after all the calls are in. In a loose game, play in this position on a good one-card draw if the opener's position is good. If other players call, you will have good odds. When the opener's position is bad, as when he is under the gun, his bet may indicate strength and you may therefore want to fold a one-card draw or a mediocre pat hand.

When the opener sits across the table, you will be in a middling position. What you play and how you play it should depend on whether anyone calls or raises the bet in front of you and on your guess of what the players behind you will do. Again, the opener's position in relation to the dealer can sometimes tell you a great deal about his holding, if you know that he knows something about position.

Position in relation to type of player. Because by far your most favorable calling position shapes up when the pot is opened to your immediate left, it is to your advantage to have on your left a player who frequently opens. On the other hand, anyone who opens on your right will put you in an unfavorable calling or raising position both before and after the draw. In general, then, you want all the eager openers lined up to your left; the sandbaggers, to your right.

It is also highly desirable to have on your left the players who bet off moderately but who seldom raise. A heavy bettor or a frequent raiser on your left will drive out the players, in addition to costing you more to play. It is best to have the raiser and the bulldozer on your right, so that you will know what he is going to do before you put your money into the pot on marginal calls.

Of course you don't always have control of where the players sit. But when the game begins, or when you drop in late, you can sometimes choose a favorable seat.

Position in relation to money distribution. Sometimes in table stakes where some players will have taller stacks than the rest, your position in relation to money distribution becomes important. If you are playing short money, it doesn't make much difference where you sit in relation to the tall stacks. But if you yourself have a lot of money before you, it is generally best to have the other loaded players on your right, so that they will have to act on their hands first (more often than not). When they make a large bet or tap, you can throw in your hand, unless it is worth calling on, without having wasted a smaller bet or call. When you tap from this position, the other loaded players on your right will often have already put some money into the pot on mediocre hands.

♥ ♥ ♥

I have assumed in the discussion above that there are no restrictions on checking before the draw. Rules against checking and raising, along with some other special rules, severely limit one's play of position. I'm obviously against such rules, but of course I abide by them when I play with groups that prefer them.

Position in Relationship to the Dealer

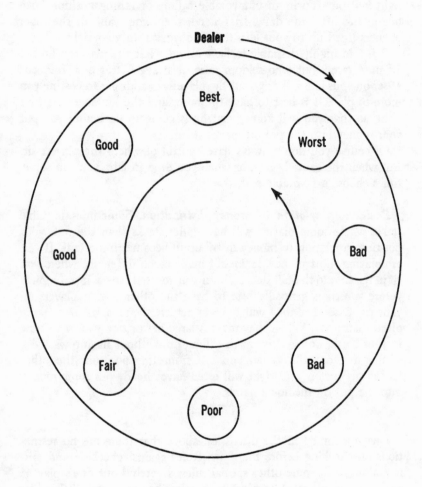

Position in Relation to Opener or First Bettor

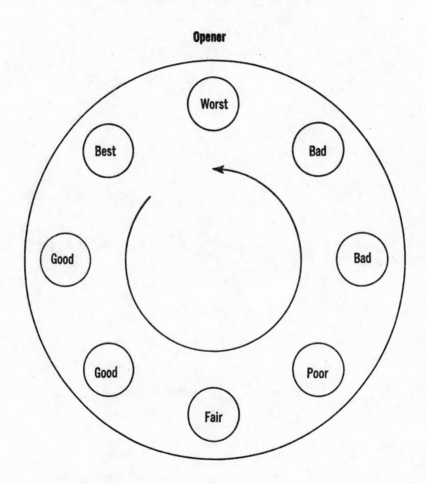

Raising Position to Drive Players Out

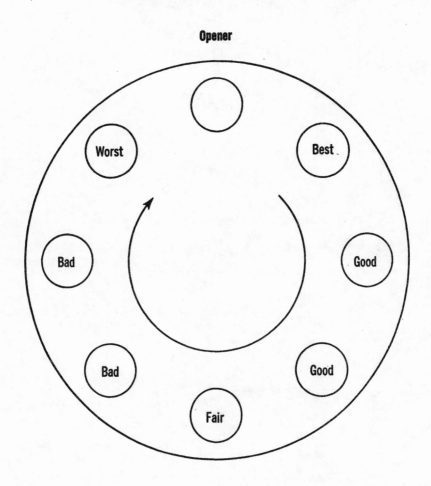

Raising Position to Build Pot

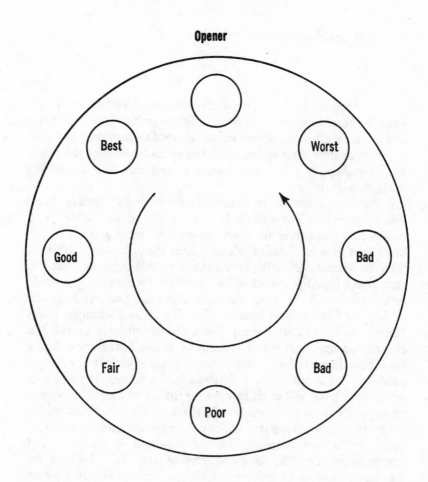

6.

Carding

Anyone who folds a fourflush before the draw because the pot doesn't offer the proper odds already understands at least one aspect of carding. Most poker players would improve their carding *and* their ability to analyze their opponent's hand by understanding the principles of probability (or at least having a familiarity with the tables) set forth in Part Two.

Particular applications of estimated carding probability are almost infinite in poker. The trouble is that it's almost impossible to remember all the figures for every situation in every game, and you don't have time for detailed calculations at the poker table. It's best, then, to concentrate on the games that are dealt more frequently in your group. If you play a lot of Deuces Wild, for instance, you could determine from Table I that there are about 2½ times as many sets of four-of-a-kind as full houses. (See the carding example under "Deuces Wild" in Part Three.) When you bet off in Jacks with trip aces and an opponent shows strength by raising heavily, you should know that there are 54,912 sets of triplets as compared to 19,716 pat hands—so it's about 2¾ to 1 that you hold a winner. If you play a lot of lowball, you will profit by knowing that there are about twice as many pat 8's as the total number of pat wheels, 6's, and 7's combined.

Yet, probability alone should not always govern carding decisions. There are tactical considerations for the hand in question, and strategical considerations for a long series of plays. Take, for example, the classic problem of holding a kicker in draw poker. If a player draws two cards to J-J-A, the ace is his kicker. He might hold it to make his opponents think that he has triplets, or to increase his chances of beating two pairs, kings or queens up. In either case, holding the kicker reduces the *overall* chances of improving a pair. Here are the comparative figures on the draw, expressed in probability:

Final Hand	Three Cards to a Pair	Two Cards to a Pair
Two pairs	0.160	0.172
Triplets	0.114	0.078
Full house	0.010	0.008
Four-of-a-kind	0.003	0.001
Any improvement	0.287	0.260

As the figures show, you have a better chance of improving a pair by throwing in the kicker and drawing three cards. In certain situations, however, the odds are altered empirically. If, for example, your opponent draws one card and you are pretty sure that he holds two high pairs, then you have a better chance of winning if you hold the ace kicker. You have a higher probability of making aces over, but a lower probability of making triplets or better.

Often a skilled player will mask triplets by holding a kicker, leading his opponents to believe that he holds two pairs, a fourflush, or a bobtail straight. But holding a kicker to triplets is never sound from a strictly mathematical viewpoint. Here are the comparative figures, expressed in probability:

Final Hand	Two Cards to Triplets	One Card to Triplets
Full house	0.061	0.064
Four-of-a-kind	0.043	0.021
Any improvement	0.104	0.085

The odds being what they are, it is usually better to draw to your best hand and not hold a kicker. But to hold a kicker on occasion does add a lot of deceptive value to your strategy, not only for a particular hand but also over a long series of plays. Varying your draw keeps the opposition guessing.

In some rather rare situations, it is almost a strategical coup to hold *two* kickers to a pair! Consider the following predicament. I opened with a pair of jacks, after everyone around the table had checked. One player called my bet and drew one card. I was almost certain that he was drawing to a flush or a straight (since he had not opened), and, as I well knew, he often bluffed heavily after busting a flush. I could have called his suspected bluff if he made it, but we were playing table stakes and I didn't want to risk being tapped out at that point in the game. So, instead of drawing the usual three cards to my hand or holding a single kicker (a trick my opponent would probably take into consideration) I held two kickers, thereby indicating two pairs or a triplet-kicker hand. It worked. I checked in the dark, and my opponent, having missed the flush, didn't bet a penny. My pair of jacks won the pot. But I really can't recommend such a draw except against certain players under special circumstances, usually in big-money play. Holding two kickers to a pair greatly reduces the probability of improving the pair, and it completely rules out a full house or four-of-a-kind.

An even more unusual situation arises, once in a blue moon, when you hold two small pairs and a high card. Assume that you hold 2-2-3-3-A. Another player, who has opened the pot, draws one card, indicating two pairs. If he does have two pairs, your treys over deuces aren't going to win the pot unless you make a full house on the draw. But there are only four cards in the deck (two treys and two deuces) that will make the full house—and you can draw only one card if you hold the two pairs. So, you have a better chance of beating two higher pairs if you throw in the pair of deuces and draw to the treys and ace kicker! As a result of making this unusual draw, five cards in the deck (two treys and three aces) will make you aces over or better—and you draw two cards instead of one. You also have a chance of drawing another high pair, such as kings or queens. Here are the comparative figures:

ONE CARD TO TWO PAIRS

Final Hand	Probability
Full house	0.085
Any improvement	(same)

TWO CARDS TO AN ACE AND A PAIR

Final Hand	Probability
Aces over	0.117
Other two pairs	0.055
Triplets	0.078
Full house	0.008
Four-of-a-kind	0.001
Any improvement	0.259

Before throwing away that extra pair, however, you had better be sure that your opponent *does* have two higher pairs! (In poker, a great deal of your carding strategy should depend on your opponent, how he bets, and so on. In short, you have to know your man.) I can't recommend the play against more than one opponent. In fact, I'm not going to recommend it against even a single opponent. One good reason: If I advised my readers to throw in the deuces and draw to the treys and ace, sooner or later one of them would try it. He would, of course, catch another deuce on the draw! Then he'd be gunning for me.

A more common problem arises when you hold a high pair along with four in suit. Do you keep the pair, or split it to draw for the flush? It depends. If you hold jacks and someone opened in front of you, chances are that your jacks are already beaten—but perhaps you should have avoided this predicament in the first place. If you open with, say, kings and a tight player calls behind you, then you have a problem not only of carding mathematics but also of judgment. In short, you should split the openers whenever you believe they are beaten. But if you think you have the best hand going in, then draw to the pair, not to the flush, because the best hand going in figures to win in the long run.

In a tough game with competent players, whether or not you have to declare that you are splitting openers should have a bearing on your decision. You make such a declaration at a considerable loss of strategical range, since your opponents will know exactly what you are doing.

♥ ♥ ♥

Card memory is important mainly in stud forms, and especially in Five-Card Stud, where only a few exposed cards can have a significant bearing on the strength and possibilities of your hand—and your opponent's. Table VII in Part Two shows how the number of exposed cards and their rank effect your chances of improving your hand, but knowing these figures will not be of much help if you fail to observe and remember the cards that have been folded around the board.

An obvious situation is when you have an ace in the hole in Five-Card Stud. If two aces have been folded around the board, you remember the fact and know that your chances of catching the case

one is slim. Another obvious situation is when you are playing for
a club flush in Seven-Card Stud. You will naturally keep count of
the puppyfeet that are showing around the board and those that
have been folded. Almost any competent stud player remembers
the cards that would have improved his own hand. But the expert
remembers *all* the cards. You never know when a seemingly in-
significant card folded early will become important later in the
hand.

Example: You hold (K-K)/J-7-K-2/(7) in Seven-Card Stud. Your
opponent bets on (?-?)/♣Q-♦J-♦Q-♦10/(?). You raise. He re-
raises. You've probably been watching his queens from the outset,
and if one has been folded earlier you know that he doesn't have
four ladies. A straight flush? You have, say, the ♦K in the hole,
which blocks the straight flush on one end. Has either the ♦8 or ♦9
been folded earlier? You probably don't remember, if several players have folded, because neither card would have had much significance during the early rounds of betting. If you have seen and
remembered either card, you can make the third raise. Your opponent *could* have four queens, but that's a slim chance you'll have
to take—unless he has tipped his powerhouse or you suspect foul
play. If you've also seen a queen folded, then you have a lock and
can bet the baby shoe money!

A good eye and memory for cards can make and save money for
you, but don't let it get you in trouble. In other words, don't
call a tap just because you know a player must have a case card
to win. You have to play your man as well as the cards. Consider
the following hand of Five-Card Stud: You hold (K)/A-K-6-10.
Player A, on your right, holds (?)/J-A-9-2. Player B, on your left,
holds (?)/Q-8-7-3. You're high and bet half the pot—say $25.
Player B calls, apparently on a pair of queens. Player A calls and
raises $100.

Has he got aces? You hold one and have seen one folded earlier.
The mathematical odds are high against his having an ace in
the hole. But what are the odds against him betting $100 if he didn't
have it? How good a player is he? If he has put you on kings, does
he know that you remember an ace being folded earlier? If so,
would he bluff when you know that he has to have the case ace
to win? Would he know that player B—who has already made a

bad $25 call—would feel obligated to "keep him honest" if the raise drives you out? If player A is a competent stud player, I say that he does have the case ace, and I wouldn't pay to see it. I'd want to look all right—but I'd let player B foot the bill.

♥ ♥ ♥

Some players have trouble remembering folded cards, and I confess that I am one of them. Practice and conscious effort will improve anybody's card memory, but the techniques of association will double your progress. The ♦J is easily remembered by the song "Jack O'Diamonds." The 8's are associated with the Dead Man's Hand. Some cards have popular names that will help you remember them. The ♦9, for example, is known as the Curse of Scotland. The ♠2, the Curse of Mexico. The ♣4, the Devil's Bedposts. Another effective association is to *look* at the face cards. Everybody knows that some of the jacks are one-eyed. Which ones? Look at the jacks around the board during a stud hand to see whether they have one or two eyes and you'll remember them after they have been folded.

Did you know that the ♦K has no mustache? Which one of the queens has a scepter? Which jack has two rows of curls? All the pip cards look pretty much alike, but did you know that the symmetry of the ♦ will help in remembering all the red pip cards? If you will compare the ♦5 with the ♥5, for example, you will see that some of the ♥'s have to be printed upside-down, whereas all the ♦'s are printed rightside-up. Which ace, in most popular brands of playing cards, carries the manufacturer's name?

♥ ♥ ♥

It's hard for me to let go of this chapter because one never seems to say enough about the art and science of carding. I stated earlier that carding applications are almost infinite. They do become infinite when you consider that there are dozens of dealer's choice games and that each and every poker player will react differently, in one way or another, to any one of the 2,598,960 possible poker hands. Because there are so many variables and conditions and nuances, some of the more subtle aspects of carding seem almost mystical.

Some poker players develop what seems to be a special carding sense. They have—and play—hunches. It could be some sort of ESP "mechanism" at work, but I doubt it. I think it's simply a matter of experience and talent for the game. Hunches are based, I think, on the sum of your poker knowledge, either consciously or unconsciously, and especially on how your opponents react to carding patterns and betting sequences. Perhaps the mind of a master poker player works rather like an electronic computer. It stores bits of data and information in a "subconscious memory bank"—usually unconscious but available for instant application to a poker problem. Perhaps the hunch is merely the computer readout. I have neither the way nor the inclination to prove all this, but I think the following example will show that hunches can sometimes be verified by carding and player analysis.

The dealer's choice session was seven-handed and very loose. $1 limit. The dealer called Anaconda, high-low. After the trash had been passed, I ended up with K-K-K-9-9. I felt good about the hand because aces are not usually passed, and, consequently, a full house with trip aces working is hard to come by. So I arranged my cards and rolled one of the 9's. A player across the board rolled the ♣K. Immediately I knew that I was beaten. I just knew it. The hunch came much too quickly to be the result of conscious analysis. Why did I have the hunch? One possibility is that something about the way the guy rolled the king might have set my "unconscious computer" working. Another definite possibility is that the king didn't fit the standard roll 'em back carding pattern of high hands in Anaconda; full houses usually take the high money, and this guy's king couldn't work in a full house because I had the rest of them. Before I even started a conscious analysis of the situation, I probably had at least two warning signals: Some mannerism during the roll warned me that he was loaded, and the normal carding pattern could not be fulfilled.

When he bet 50¢ my hunch became almost a conviction. He had a good hand. Something about his manner showed it as plainly as a $ sign ringing up on a cash register. He was a conservative player who seldom bluffed—at least not in this loose low-limit session—except for strategical semibluffs in games like Seven and Twenty-Seven. I had never seen him run a pure bluff from the beginning of a hand to the end, and he was a good enough player to know that anything lower than a full house was not strong in Anaconda. So, I put him on a ♣ straight flush.

Several low players called his 50¢ bet. I played along, deciding to see if his next roll did continue the straight flush. After the betting interval, I rolled a king. He rolled an off-suit queen. He didn't have the straight flush, so I had to put him on four queens now. Without even taking a second look at my exposed king, he bet a buck. I folded. A couple of raises took place before the hand was over, so I saved $6 or $7 by folding. My only regret is that I didn't save the 50¢. He turned up the fourth queen at the showdown!

7.

Swinging High, Swinging Low

Almost all poker games are played high-low from time to time in modern dealer's choice sessions. The basic principle, as the name implies, is that the high hand wins half the pot and the low hand wins the other half. It would seem, on first thought, that the high hands should be played as usual in high poker and the low hands as usual in low poker. But this is not the case.

The high hand is at a disadvantage, in most high-low games, because a lot of low hands—hands that would not normally be played in regular high poker—develop into little straights and flushes. Thus, the low hands have a tremendous advantage in a game like Seven-Card Stud High-Low because they can win both ways. This advantage is so great that playing high hands is futile in some games and variations. Consider an example:

The game is Seven-Card Stud High-Low. Pot limit, $1 ante. Player A holds (K-K)/K. Player B, (2-3)/4. Player A bets $2. Player B calls and announces a raise. There is $6 ante in the pot (assuming a six-handed game), plus A's $2 bet plus B's $2 call. So, B raises $10. Player A calls, making a total of $30 in the pot. The other players fold.

On the next serve, A catches a jack, giving him (K-K)/K-J. Player B catches a 5, giving him (2-3)/4-5. Player A checks. Player B bets the pot—$30. Player A calls, making a total of $90 in the pot.

On the next serve, A catches a 9; B, a 7. A checks, but again B bets the pot—$90. Player A calls, making a total of $270 in the pot. On the serve, A catches an ace, giving him (K-K)/K-J-9-A. Player

B also catches an ace, giving him (2-3)/4-5-7-A. He bets the pot— $270.

Player A squirms in his seat. He knows that B could have a straight. But he (A) could make kings full . . . and besides, B may be trying to bully him out of the pot. So, A calls the bet, making a total of $810 in the pot.

Player A catches a 10-spot down the river, giving him (K-K)/K-J-9-A/(10). It doesn't matter what B catches because he's already made a perfect for low and a wheel straight for high. So, B bets the $810. If A calls, there will be a total of $2430 in the pot.

Player A finally calls. He loses high. He loses low. All together, he has put more than $1200 in the pot. If he had filled up, he would have gotten his money back. But what did he stand to *win?* Half the ante. Exactly $3.

What should player A have done with his three kings? He should have folded them, fast, at the outset!

Of course, the example above is an extreme case. But it does illustrate what the split-pot principle can do to the odds on high hands. Consider a similar example with three players—two low and one high hand containing (K-K)/K. It's a fixed limit game and each player puts a total of $20 into the pot. At worst, the three kings can lose both ways. At best, the three kings can split the pot and *win* $10. (That is, the player put $20 into the pot and got back $30.) If the game had been high only, the trip kings could have won $40.

Obviously, when you play high in high-low you should figure the odds on half the pot—and remember that you'll sometimes be clobbered by a sorry looking high hand, such as (2-3)/7, which would not have been played in regular high poker. Thus, the high hands have *more* competition and *less* potential gain in high-low as compared to regular high poker.

The cardinal rule for winning play in high-low, then, is to play only low hands. But, stated thus, this rule sounds a little too defensive, or restrictive, whereas at the poker table there is a no more aggressive player than one who has low cinched and an opportunity for high as well. So I'll change the rule to: Play hands that can win both ways.

I feel so strongly about this rule that I will repeat it in more emphatic type:

PLAY HANDS THAT CAN WIN BOTH WAYS.

Since dozens of games are played high-low, for stakes ranging from penny ante to no limit, there are bound to be exceptions. Some of the characteristics and quirks of the particular games are discussed in Part Three. Other exceptions occur because high-low is complicated by different methods of showdown or declaration, in which the players have to announce whether they are contending for high, for low, or for both.

The more commonly used methods of declaration are *cards speak for themselves* (shortened to *cards speak*), *simultaneous declaration* (usually called *chips declare*), and *consecutive declaration* (sometimes called *position declare*). Each method requires different strategy and tactics as well as having a definite bearing on playing requirements.

In cards speak, the showdown takes place as in any other form of poker. The best high hand and the best low hand split the pot automatically without any sort of declaration. Quite often one player will have a good hand both ways, in which case he may win all the pot. In Cincinnati High-Low, for example, it's entirely possible for a player to have a wheel for low and a full house for high.

Generally, cards speak is the easiest to play of the three methods of declaration. The cardinal rule—play low—should be applied more firmly in cards speak than in chips declare or position declare. Although cards speak doesn't require the sort of cunning analysis and educated guesswork required of the expert chips declare player, or the positional jockeying of the position declare player, it is the safest method for the percentage man. It is a different game, really, from chips and position declare, as will be made clear in an example following brief discussions of the other methods of declaration.

In chips declare, each active player must declare whether he is going for high, for low, or for both. This is accomplished by each active player concealing a certain number of chips or coins in his hand. Then all active players reveal their chips simultaneously. (In most circles, two chips indicate that you are playing both ways. One chip, high. No chip, low. A few groups use different colored chips to indicate high, low, or both ways.) Most players will take at least two chips in their hands, put both hands under the table, secretly put the proper number in their right hand, place their right fist on the table, and open up simultaneously with the other active players.

When every active player declares the same way, the best hand in that direction wins all the pot. In other words, there is no low money when every player declares high, and no high money when every player declares low. If a player decides to swing, he must *win* both ways to get any of the pot; he loses *both* ways if he loses or ties *either* way.

The ability to determine which way the opposition is going characterizes the expert chips declare player, and some players develop a talent for backing in—winning by declaring high on a low hand, or low on a high hand.

The swing requirements bring about some unusual situations in which a player can win half the pot on a sorry hand even when he has strong opposition. Such a case occurs when a player swings and is beaten or tied one way or the other. For example, you hold three aces for high. Player A swings on 7-6-5-4-3 and player B declares low with 6-4-3-2-A. Since A loses for low, he also loses high—and you get half the pot. If both A and B made wheels and both decided to swing, you would win *all* the money on trip aces, a hand that wouldn't have got you a penny either way in cards speak!

In consecutive declaration, the last bettor or raiser must declare first. If the last round of betting is checked out, the high man must declare first. Then the players declare in turn behind him, clockwise. When a player announces that he is trying for both high and low, he must win both ways to win either way.

Consecutive declaration is a game of position, in which the good hands will often sandbag and the sorry hands will sometimes bet. If you hold a very good hand, and especially one that is concealed, you will want to be the last player to declare in hopes that the others will go the same way. Such a hand in Seven-Card Stud High-Low would be (A-A)/A-3-6-5/(6). This hand looks very low to the opposition but is really a concealed powerhouse for high. In an early position, you would have to declare high, thereby giving a player in a later position the opportunity to back in for low. If you are the last to speak, however, all the other players may well go high in front of you, especially if no one has connected on a good low hand.

Sometimes, however, it is to your advantage to declare first when you have more than one opponent. If you hold (4-Q)/A-3-4-6/(K), you don't have a decent hand either way, but you look very low; the proper play here is to indicate strength by betting or raising, thereby putting yourself in position to declare first. You may convince a candidate for low to try to back in for high or you may convince a potential swing hand (such as 8-7-6-5-4) to be content with high money. The success of such a play will depend on what sort of low hands are out and on how good—or bad—the opponents are. You may be called by very good players, who may see through your strategy, or by very poor players, who pay scant attention to positional matters.

♥ ♥ ♥

A running example will point up some of the characteristics of the different methods of declaration, as well as illustrate the playing tactics and problems of each method. Let the game be Seven-Card Stud High-Low with you and one other active player at the showdown.

You Hold	Player A Holds
(2-3)/4-8-3-10/(3)	(?-?)/♦6-♠A-♥6-♣J/(?)

In cards speak, you have a lock one way or the other—but you don't know which way. If player A holds trip 6's or better, you win low money with your 10-8-4-3-2. If he has a good low hand, you win high money with your trip treys. Analyze the possibilities of A's hand closely and you'll see that he can't possibly have better than a jack-low if he has trip 6's or better for high, and that he can't have a flush or straight. Because you have a lock one way or the other, you can bet the maximum limit. In pot limit, bet it. In table stakes, tap. You have a chance to win all the pot if A folds, and can possibly win it all even if he calls. Note that if A has an ace in the hole, a jack is the best he can do for low. So, you have low money. He would have two pairs, aces over 6's, for high. So, you win the high money.

Your hand is not strong either way—yet you can freely tap on it in cards speak. But you couldn't tap in chips declare—and may not be able to call if *he* taps. He could easily have a hand lower than 10-8, possibly even a sixty-four. He could easily have trip 6's or better for high. Since your hand isn't a powerhouse either way, you'll have to guess which way to go. If player A shows weakness by checking, you may decide to swing. But is he really weak, or did he check to try to induce you to swing into his full house or sixty-four? Such sandbagging during the latter rounds of betting is quite common, among the better players, in chips declare.

What happens when player A shows much strength by betting heavily? Such a bet would indicate that he is strong one way or the other. You may not have a call—and may have to fold a hand that you could tap on in cards speak! Whether or not you call should depend on the size of the pot in relation to A's bet. If the pot contains $20 in table stakes and he taps for $100, you should bow out. If you called, you'd be sending $100 after $10 (half the pot before the tap). In other words, you'd be laying 10 to 1 odds that you could guess which way he is going. In pot limit, he could bet only $20; if you call, you'll be laying 2 to 1 that you can guess which way he's going. You may have a call in pot limit, however, if you know your man (he may almost always start out playing for low, for example) and if you remember the cards that have been folded, and if you have some idea, based on the history of the betting, which way he is going. When you're playing $2 limit, you definitely have a call because you'd be sending $2 after $10 and you have a 50-50 chance of winning even if your decision to go high or low is reduced to a pure guess.

Obviously, there is a world of difference between cards speak and chips declare. Consecutive declaration presents other opportunities —and other problems. Your position can become so important in consecutive declaration that it sometimes determines whether you call or fold. The same example used for cards speak and chips declare will illustrate the importance of position. If you'll look again at the hands, you'll see that player A is high man with a pair of 6's showing. If he bets, you can call. You can call even a tap bet because you have a winner one way or the other. When he declares, you simply go the other way. If he bet and you raised, however, or if he checked and you bet, you will have to declare first and could lose all the pot if you guess wrong.

♥   ♥   ♥

Note that the high hand can win all the money in both chips declare and consecutive declaration. This possibility has an effect on playable hands—at least theoretically. Although high triplets that fill up will sometimes get all the pot from swinging straights and flushes, you do not usually have much deception with such hands. A holding like (K-K)/K is pegged high at the outset. So, I still say that good low hands with high potential make by far the best bet in most (but not all) high-low games, no matter which method of declaration is used.

But I'm not categorically against playing high hands in chips declare or consecutive declaration. In fact, one of the biggest pots I ever won was on a high hand in Seven-Card Stud High-Low. After the last hole card had been dealt out, I held (2-2)/A-2-3-6/(2). My opponent for low showed (?-?)/4-5-7-10/(?). A high man had been betting all the way on (?-?)/Q-9-J-J/(?). He bet off again during the last betting interval. The low man called. I tapped. The high man called. The low man quit. Much to the high man's surprise, I declared high with one chip and beat his queens full with my four deuces. I want to emphasize, however, that my high hand was effectively concealed and that I was very much in the race for low money until the last card fell.

High-low is further complicated because there are three scales for low, as discussed under "Low Poker" in Part Three. In one scale, straights and flushes bust a low hand, so that A-2-3-4-6 in mixed suits is the best possible low. In another scale, aces, straights, and flushes count high, so that 7-5-4-3-2 in mixed suits is the best possible low. In the other scale, called California Lowball, aces can be played either high or low and so can straights and flushes, so that A-2-3-4-5 is the best possible low as well as being a straight for high.

California Lowball is becoming more and more popular, and I prefer it in most high-low games because it gets more action at the table by increasing the number of potential swing hands. The greater number and frequency of swinging hands affords more opportunities for the expert player to exercise his skill—and presents more pitfalls for the haphazard swinger.

Knowing when to swing and when to be content with half the pot seems to be an uncanny sixth sense with the expert high-low player. Ability—skill—talent—whatever it is may well be the most important decision-making faculty in modern poker. The stakes are high. When you decide to swing in a $1 limit game, you are risking much, much more than the maximum bet. When you have a cinch for half a $40 pot and decide to swing for the other half, you are in effect betting $20 that you can beat your opponent.

To swing or not to swing isn't, or shouldn't be, a snap end-play decision. The expert, when playing for the wheel or sixty-four flush, will have been analyzing his opponents and their cards throughout the hand. A knowledge of one's opponent, along with the betting and carding history of the hand in question, will usually be more reliable at the showdown than purely mathematical considerations.

Swing decisions are very often influenced by the quirks and peculiarities of the particular high-low games. The expert will know, for example, that tie wheels are not at all uncommon in Baseball High-Low; consequently, he will be very careful about swinging in this particular game. He will know that a flush isn't likely to win high money in Cincinnati High-Low whenever a pair shows in the widow, and so on.

A good many high-low games and variations are discussed in Part Three. If you play a particular high-low game that isn't discussed in Part Three, or isn't discussed in enough detail, I advise you to deal out a few hundred hands. This will take a little time—but it will probably pay off in cold cash at an impressive hourly wage!

8.

Playing the Widow

I dealt myself the ace and the king of diamonds. The player under the gun opened for $1. Several others called. A professional poker man on my right raised $10. Because it would be better, I thought, to have one opponent call a $30 bet than to have three call a $10 bet, I raised another $20. The players folded around the table like a circle of dominoes. Except for the pro. He tapped.

I didn't know how much money he had in his stack, but it stood three inches tall with at least one $100-bill on the bottom. We were playing table stakes, though, and the pro had no doubt sized up my own little stack before pushing all that money into the pot. Even so, I had nearly $100 left—a bet sizable enough to give me pause.

I looked again at my two hole cards. The ace and the king were still there and still red. I liked them. Having played a lot of stud poker, I knew that the combination had good possibilities. Trouble was, we weren't playing stud.

They called the game Hold Me Darling, or Hold Me for short. Each player received two cards face down. A round of betting followed. Then three communal cards were turned up in the middle. Another bet. Another turn card. Another bet. Final turn card. Final bet. Showdown. Simple enough? Well, yes, mechanically. But strategically and mathematically it was different from any poker game I had ever run up against.

I counted the money in my little stack. I counted the money in the pot. If I called, I would be sending nearly $100 after about $150. Was my ace-king combination worth the gamble? What did my op-

ponent hold? A pair. I had to put him on a high pair. Because
I held one of the aces and one of the kings, I put him on queens.
If he did hold queens, there were only two cards in the deck—
the other queens—that would help his hand on the turn. Six cards
—three aces and three kings—would make me a pair higher than
queens. My hand had the better chance of improving. But the
pro didn't necessarily have to improve to beat me. Even if I had
guessed his hand correctly, I still didn't know whether I had a
good gamble. In short, I didn't know what I was doing.

"On you, Livingston," somebody said, scowling at me for delay-
ing the game.

I had sat in on this session not to whisk that crew to the cleaners
at their own game but to play niggardly while learning something
about Hold Me, which, in a very short time, had dominated much of
the high-stakes action in my area. But my present fix convinced
me that I had a lot to learn about the game before I would be
ready for combat.

"Take the pot," I said, dealing off the turn cards. The last one
was a king, and I slapped it down onto the table. The pro grinned
and showed me two black queens. I would have won! But had I had
a good gamble?

At home, I went through my library of poker books. None of them
covered Hold Me, or any game like it under another name. No-
where could I find any figures on the odds and probabilities. So, out
came my slide rule and scratch pad.

On the basis of my calculations, I determined that I had had a
0.44+ probability of winning with my A-K. But I knew that
mathematicians as renowned as d'Alembert have gone astray on
problems of probability. To test my figures, I pitted the A-K against
the black queens and dealt out a thousand hands. The queens
won 527 times; the A-K, 467 times; and there were 6 ties. A probability of 0.44 meant that I should win 440 some-odd hands out of
1,000, so my figures checked as closely as could be expected.

Clearly, the queens had a slight edge over the A-K. But that does
not necessarily mean that I should have folded. The pot offered odds
of 150 to 100 (roughly), or 1½ to 1. With a win probability of
0.4, the correct odds would be $4/(10-4)$ to 1, or 1½ to 1! Whether
or not to call, then, was a toss-up.

The plain truth is that in a loose Hold Me session with a dozen players, a tightwad could not pick two cards from the deck that would give him a usurious percentage edge before the turn. (I am *not* recommending that Hold Me players see the turn come hell or high water. As in most other poker games, high cards will win more pots; but low cards, when they come through, will often win bigger pots.)

After the turn, however, the somewhat topsy-turvy character of Hold Me changes. The A-K vs. Q-Q does not fully illustrate the subtlety of the game because the tap-out before the turn reduced my decision to mere mathematics. Another high-stakes hand, also played by a professional, will be in order here. Before giving a play-by-play account, however, I had better clear up a point.

Draw poker players will have raised their eyebrows at my mentioning a twelve-handed poker game. In draw poker and Seven-Card Stud, there aren't enough cards to play more than eight-handed. Because each player receives only two down-cards in Hold Me, twenty or more players can sit in—if the table is big enough. I have played fourteen-handed.

In my favorite poker circle, whose nucleus was a bunch of missile and rocket engineers, Hold Me became so popular that the guys chipped in to build a bigger table. More and more players huddled in, bringing more and more cash, until a highly undesirable character fingered the game for heisters. (Two of them came in one night with pistols and a sawed-off shotgun.) After that event, we floated the game for a while, but it was never quite the same. Finally the group fell apart. The table ended up in an even bigger Hold Me game, held each week in a motel by a professional gambler. The cops raided the game, and the local press made a front-page photograph of our big Hold Me table!

Anyway, the number of players does have a bearing on the game. As in other forms of poker, the more players at the table, the greater the element of luck; at the same time, a large number of players in Hold Me makes the game a percentage man's meat. With a dozen or so players at the table, even inside straights are frequently worth a gamble; just as conditioned stud players consider pip cards to be trash, draw players in a Hold Me session usually consider inside straights to be a sucker's play. Sometimes they are, too. Remember the story about the poker-playing farmer who lost the back forty by drawing to inside straights, and lost the rest of the farm when he finally hit one? The moral of the story applies to Hold Me whenever a pair shows in the widow, as the following hand illustrates.

The pro had a pair of 7's going in. The bet was small—$5—so he played along. I called on two court cards. Several others called. The dealer, an intelligent bookmaker, burned the top card (a common practice in high-stakes play) and turned 4-6-7. Having concealed triplets now, the pro bet the size of the pot—about $35. I threw in my court cards, since I hadn't paired on the turn. A gambler who played like a monkey called. The bookie called, then dealt. The turn card was a 6, making 4-6-7-6 in the widow and giving the pro a full house.

He bet $50. The monkey called. The bookie called.

The final turn card was a 5, making a bobtail straight in the widow. The pro bet $100. The monkey raised $100. Without hesitation, the bookie called. The pro raised another $300. The monkey called. The bookie tapped!

The pro smiled off his bad luck, then tossed his two 7's onto the deadwood pile. The monkey called what he could of the tap bet. Then the bookie turned over a pair of 6's, which, with the two on the board, made him four-of-a-kind. Broke now, the monkey said, "I *had* to call on a straight." He had called simply because he had made the straight, and no reasonable amount of money would have made him throw it away. To call had been almost a point of honor.

The pro, on the other hand, threw in because he knew that a full house is no better than a pair of deuces if it doesn't win the pot. How did he know it wouldn't win? On a hunch? No. He analyzed the play.

Being the dealer, the bookie had the best possible position at the table because he was the last to act on his hand. If he had held two high cards, in this ideal position, he would have raised before the turn. Moreover, the bookie would not have called the opening bet with a big card and a little card, unless they happened to be an ace-pip in suit. Chances were, then, that the bookie held either a small pair or two small straight cards. The betting sequence, and especially the tap, indicated a pair of 6's down. Of utmost importance was the pro's knowledge of the bookie's character. If the bookie had been another monkey, the pro would probably have called the tap. But the bookie was cagey enough to sandbag. He was also cautious and would not have tapped without holding a lock. He was intelligent, and no doubt he had subjected the pro's hand to analysis; before deciding to sandbag during the last betting interval, he had to have put the pro on a full house.

How did the pro know that the bookie wasn't bluffing? That was the easiest part of the analysis. The bookie might conceivably have bluffed against the pro or another good player, but never against the monkey. The bookie knew that the monkey would call, and the pro knew that he knew it.

The point here is not to buck the odds by trying to make a hero out of a man who threw in a full house but to illustrate the precision with which a Hold Me hand can be analyzed. It is a great game.

Exactly how widely Hold Me has spread is difficult to determine, partly because it is known by different names. The reports that I have received, however, indicate that the game has pretty much covered the country, although many social groups that play for low stakes might not have heard of it. The game seems to be more popular in high-stakes play than in the 25¢ limit class. While writing an article on the game for *Life* magazine (on which this chapter is based), I called a poker man in Colorado and asked whether Hold Me Darling was being dealt out there. "Never heard of it," he said. "But a new game has really caught on. High Hold'em. Each player gets two down cards. You bet on 'em. Then three cards are turned up in the middle. . . ."

♥ ♥ ♥

In American poker, the standard big-money game for the past fifty years has been Five-Card Stud. According to Albert H. Morehead, "Thirty years ago two-thirds of the professional games were Five-Card Stud; today, not one-tenth are." In spite of the current popularity of high-low and the bulldog hold of draw, the passing of stud has left a void in the poker world. Hold Me or some similar game—such as Omaha or Amarillo—may fill it.

One reason, I think, is that Hold Me offers a feature of Five-

Card Stud that is very important to serious poker players. In stud, an expert player can tell pretty much where he stands; when the cards are up at the end of *every* deal, he can tell whether he holds a lock. If, for example, a player has two pairs and no other pair, no fourflush, or no possible straight shows around the board, then he can bet the baby shoe money. To have a lock in straight draw poker, one would have to hold a royal flush, which is a once a lifetime hand. Similarly, in Seven-Card Stud it is usually difficult to tell whether one holds a lock; an opponent can end up with a full house or four-of-a-kind without a single pair showing. But in Hold Me, as in Five-Card Stud, it is possible to tell whether one has a lock after the cards are up. If, for example, a player holds the ♣A-3, then he holds a mortal lock if three ♣'s show in the middle, providing that no pair shows and that the three communal ♣'s are not open to a straight flush.

The main reason for Hold Me's popularity is the play it gets at the table. In fact, the trend in poker has always been toward more and more action.

In the original form of poker, each player received five cards face-down. There was no draw, and only one betting interval took place. The draw was introduced to liven up the game by adding another betting interval and to make room for strategy. During the War Between the States, or thereabouts, a radical new form of poker came along—stud. Lowball gained widespread popularity during World War II, but this innovation was a reversal of standard poker's hierarchical scale, not a new form. Then high-low came like a tidal wave blown in by Tyche, goddess of fortune; even now, though, high-low shows signs of recession, simply because those who like the game have learned to play only for low (in most variations) or else they have gone broke. Again, high-low is not a new form of poker.

But a new form—widow poker—has taken shape gradually. Perhaps its archetype was Spit-in-the-Ocean, in which a communal card is turned up in the middle. Other widow games followed: Cincinnati, Hollywood, Southern Cross, X-Marks-the-Spot, Bedsprings. Until Hold Me came along, all these widow games were too unpredictable for comfort in high-stakes play. Hold Me, then, may be a culmination of a new form. I believe that it may be a major event in the history of poker, and I predict that it will all but replace Five-Card Stud for the rest of the century.

One reason for the passing of stud is that people learned how to play it. There is a story about a tight old stud man who simply would not stay in unless he had an ace in the hole. His opponents copped all the aces from the deck, and the old fellow sat there until he anted himself broke! If properly played, Five-Card Stud can be almost that drab. Actually, Hold Me is more lively than stud ever was, partly because of the increased play of straights and flushes. Any respectable stud man would quickly fold ♠5-6, but such pip cards in suit are often worth a call in Hold Me.

What are the best two cards that a player can have before the turn in Hold Me? In a twelve-handed game, I would choose 10-J of the same suit; in a five-handed game, a pair of aces. The trouble with a pair in the hole is that only two cards in the deck will improve your hand without helping the rest of the players too.

The truth is that each hand of Hold Me is different, and there is no established "par." A good deal depends on the first three turn cards. Hand in and hand out during a long period of play, however, the real key to the game is what Hold Me players call *overlays* and kickers. But the full importance of overlays won't become clear until pairs have been discussed.

Hold Me is one game—along with similar widow games—in which a pair is not just a pair! Which is better, a pair of 10's in the hole or a pair of 10's with one in the hole and one in the widow? The split pair is by far the better holding, in spite of the fact that triplets made with a pair in the hole could be concealed. Only two cards in the deck will improve a pair of 10's in the hole without improving the communal widow. With one 10 down and one in the widow, *five* cards will improve the hand—two 10's plus three cards of the same rank as the other hole card. Moreover, a 10 in the widow would be less likely to improve your opponent's hands than another card; in other words, (10-J) down and 10-2-3 in the widow would be more likely to hold up than (10-10) down and J-2-3 in the widow because the jack would be more likely to help your opponents than the 10 would.

Even though a split pair is far better than a pair in the hole, a split pair is not just a split pair! Much depends on the other turn cards. Sometimes an expert Hold Me player will raise on split tens; at other times he will be quick to fold them. He will raise or bet vigorously when he holds (10-K) in his hand and 10-2-3 turn up in the widow; but he will sometimes fold when he holds (10-8) down and A-K-10 turn up in the widow, because if there are several active players one or more of them is likely to have an ace or a king in the hole. In other words, the value of the split pair is determined in part by how many *overlays* are out.

The value of a split pair is also determined by the rank of the kicker. Thus, (10-A) down and 10-6-5 in the widow is worth a raise, but (10-2) down and 10-6-5 is worth only a call and should usually be folded if the play indicates that an opponent also holds a pair of 10's (or better). His higher kicker gives him a big advantage. In this case, only three cards (three deuces) would improve the (10-2) hand without also improving the (10-A) hand, and of course the (10-A) would have the same chance of improving *but would not necessarily have to improve to win.* Note that another 10 turned up in the widow would merely get the (10-2) hand in deeper water! Another pair turned up in the widow would merely improve both hands, and the ace kicker would still have the big advantage.

Paradoxically, it is often better for you if your opponent holds two pairs instead of a higher pair and a kicker! Assume that you hold (10-2) down and 10-6-5 show in the widow. If your opponent holds (10-A), only three cards (the deuces) will give you a winner. Even if you make a deuce he can still win by catching any one of nine cards—three aces, three 6's, and three 5's. But if your opponent holds (6-5) down, you have three deuces and two 10's— plus the possibility of another pair in the widow—that would give you a winner. If you do hit one of these cards, only one of two 6's or two 5's would put him out front, as compared to nine cards with the (10-A) holding!

The points I've brought out above also apply to Omaha or Amarillo. These two widow games are similar to Hold Me, in that each player ends up with two hole cards and five communal up cards. Yet, they are vastly different, have different staying requirements, and require different strategy for winning play! These games are discussed and contrasted to Hold Me in Part Three.

9.

Dealing with Cheats

A dealer who is adept at manipulating a deck of playing cards in one way or another is called a mechanic. A mechanic who specializes in dealing the second card in the deck—thereby saving the top card for himself or an accomplice—is called a number-two man. If the truth be known, accomplished number-two men probably outnumber really skilled cellar men, who specialize in dealing from the bottom of the deck.

I am reluctant to buck the popularity of the phrase "dealing from the bottom." Yet, there are explainable reasons why the unsung number-two man is really the number-one card mechanic, not in fiction or movies or TV, but at the poker table.

First, consider marked cards. They are all but useless in the cellar dealer's art as such, simply because markings on the backs of the bottom cards would not be in view. The number-two man, on the other hand, has the back of the top card in plain view, and he can save it for himself or give it to any player at the table.

Second, the bottom card remains fixed until the cellar dealer takes it. But the top card changes continuously during the course of a legitimate deal. Thus, the number-two man has a choice of distribution on a number of cards. In a seven-handed game of Jacks, for instance, he sees as many as 35 "top" cards before the draw.

Third, casino blackjack created a demand for skilled number-two men, but not especially for cellar dealers, who are foiled by the burned cards on the bottom of the deck.

Fourth, the number-two man need not necessarily resort to premarked cards, which are concrete evidence of cheating. Moreover, he `doesn't have to stack the deck, nullify the cut, and so on. Most second dealers specializing in blackjack and Five-Card Stud (where the hole card is often all-important) turn a profit merely by peeking at the top card. Peeking can be accomplished by several ways, but it is usually done while the dealer pretends to check his hole card.

Fifth, the number-two man can achieve a smoothness that is probably hard for the cellar dealer to match. If the number-two man has talent and if he practices enough in front of a mirror, he can perfect his coordination to such a degree that his second dealing is impossible to see with the naked eye.

Usually, a number-two man holds the deck firmly in his left hand. In a normal deal, he pushes out the top card with his left thumb and takes it with his right hand for the serve. When he chooses to deal the second card, he still pushes out the top card with his left thumb; but his thumb then retracts the top card while his right hand takes the second card. Actually, by exquisite control of pressure and movement, he can make the second card protrude an eighth of an inch before he retracts the top card, thereby making the operation smoother. If he is not accomplished enough to start the second card moving out, he must sort of hit the deck with his right thumb after he has retracted the top card.

Although the ruse cannot be detected with the eye if it is properly done, there are several tip-offs to watch for if you suspect someone of dealing seconds. First, notice the way the dealer holds the cards. Most number-two men use the standard mechanic's grip, in which the slightly beveled deck is held deep in the left palm. The index finger curls along the end of the pack, and the other three fingers crook around the long edge. But bear in mind that because a dealer holds the cards in this way does not necessarily brand him as a number-two man. Also, holding the deck another way does not preclude second dealing. In fact, it's possible to deal seconds with one hand!

Second, listen for the telltale swish. The second card, in contact with both the top and third cards, makes a slightly different sound from a normal deal. The intensity of this sound is inversely proportional to the mechanic's skill.

Third, watch the left thumb. In a normal deal, it will lift up slightly after pushing out the top card. But while dealing seconds, the mechanic's thumb will stay in contact with the top card as he pushes it out and then retracts it.

Fourth, watch the man who shows a marked preference for a certain kind of cards. It is harder to deal seconds with cards that have a white border (such as Bicycle) than with cards having an overall pattern (such as Bee). Also, it is harder to deal good seconds with plastic cards than with pasteboards.

Fifth, inspect the cards for markings, paying attention to the left top corners. Also, play light off the cards at different angles while looking for thumbnail indentations, creases, or peg bumps; again, pay particular attention to the top left corners. Be especially suspicious of offbeat brands of playing cards, which could be factory marked.

Sixth, be a little wary of the man who always deals Five-Card Stud. This game is of course an old standby—but for cheats as well as diehard stud players.

Seventh, beware of the man who deals with one hand and seems to throw the cards to the players around the table. A one-handed deal is both unnatural and unnecessary.

I want to emphasize that these tip-offs do not prove that a man is dealing seconds. But if your suspect seldom loses and does show some of the tip-offs, then I think you are justified in being highly suspicious of him. Remember also that a really slick mechanic will not usually cheat every time he gets his hands on the deck. Once or twice a night is enough.

Perhaps the best safeguard against seconds and other forms of cheating is not to play with strangers. A friend of mine told me, after listening to me hold forth at some length about seconds, that he wouldn't play poker for high stakes with *anybody*, friend or stranger, unless they used a dealing box. "Then you'd really be asking for trouble," I said. "Only a skilled mechanic can deal seconds competently with his hands, but any jackleg cheat can do it to you with a gaffed dealing box!"

♥ ♥ ♥

That some familiar brands of playing cards turn out to be marked, or tampered with in one way or another, does not asperse the card manufacturers. Playing cards, contrary to popular belief, are not marked during the manufacturing process. (A few offbeat patterns, such as clock-dial designs, are marked when they are printed, but neither the knowledgeable poker player nor the professional card cheat would have any truck with these.) The reputable manufacturers of popular brands of playing cards do not mark, deface, trim, or sort their product.

Playing cards can be marked or otherwise doctored by the cheat himself, but the large-scale work is done by the gambling supply houses. Skilled employees at these houses remove all wrappings, seals, and revenue stamps from legitimate decks, which are purchased by the gross. After doctoring the cards in one way or another, they carefully rewrap, reseal, and restamp the decks. The repackaged cards, and a number of other crooked gambling devices, are sold regularly through "magic shops" or directly to cheats.

The terms explained below give only an indication of the ways that have been devised to mark or doctor cards:

Cosmetics. Marking or shading the backs of playing cards by using various kinds of gook and ink is sometimes called cosmetics. Dozens of concoctions are available from the gaff supply houses, including luminous inks, pencils, and daubs for making luminous readers (discussed later). Generally, the daub leaves a slight smudge, or shade, on the back of the cards. Cosmetics is usually practiced by the cheat during play, and commercial daubers, or shading boxes, are designed to be attached to the cheat's clothing.

Blue aniline pencils have been used in daubing, and so have cigar ashes. A wax will slick up the backs of aces and other key cards, thereby enabling the mechanic to locate them by a cut or by breaks in the deck—and there is a special "roughing" compound that will make cards more resistant. Also, special ink is used to mark the edge of playing cards.

Border Work. This term refers to markings put on cards by inking a slight hump on the top left and bottom right corners of the borders. (Several popular brands, such as Bicycle, have white borders between the design and the edge of the card; other brands, such as Bee, have patterns that cover the entire back.) Usually, a mark high toward the top indicates an ace; a slightly lower mark, a king; and so on. Also, some cards, such as Bicycle, have a small inner border, or a white strip, than can be used for markings.

Border work makes ideal markings for second dealers because the mark on the top card can be seen readily when the cards are beveled in the standard mechanic's grip. On the other hand, border work is relatively easy for a keen-eyed player to spot; consequently, the really accomplished mechanic will probably avoid such markings.

Sorts. When playing cards are cut with a die during the manufacturing process, there are inevitably slight and numerous variations along the edges of the back pattern. Because these variations are numerous and random in each legitimate deck, such imperfections are of no value to the cheat or mechanic. But if the cheat buys a number of decks, and if he has enough time, he can sort one deck in which the pattern edge variations will not be random.

Instead of making up his own sorts, the cheat can purchase them from the gaff supply houses, which buy many gross of decks and hire girls to pigeonhole key cards that show similar pattern edge variations. Also, the cheat or the gaff supply houses can fake sorts by trimming certain cards slightly. But fake sorts are dangerous for the cheat because they can be detected, whereas true sorts are considered to be the safest of marked cards because they are not actually marked.

Cards that have a white border can be used in the same way as fake sorts if the edges of the key cards are trimmed enough to make for readable variations in the margin.

Sunning the Deck. A method of shading key cards by placing them in strong sunlight for a few hours.

Belly Strippers. There are several kinds of strippers, all of which have been cut or trimmed into one shape or another. Usually, a thirty-second of an inch is trimmed from the sides or ends of all the cards except the key cards (aces, kings, etc, as the cheat chooses). Then the key cards are cut separately so that they are larger on one end, or convex, or concave. After the cards have been trimmed, their corners are rerounded.

Belly strippers, or humps, are the most commonly used of all the strippers. They are made by cutting a thirty-second of an inch off both sides of each card except the key cards. The key cards are then cut convexly on both long sides, so that a slight belly protrudes about the middle. Other kinds of strippers are tapered toward one end, and still others are trimmed concavely. End strippers are cut on the ends rather than on the long sides. Combinations of end and side strippers are possible. Also, the mechanic might use just one stripper to facilitate cutting to a card or portion of the deck; such a single stripper is called a brief.

The gaff supply houses sell dozens of variations of strippers. Also, they sell precision trimming equipment for the do-it-yourself enthusiast!

Luminous Readers. Red cards marked with green luminous ink that is invisible to the naked eye but brazenly visible with the aid of tinted glasses or visors are called luminous readers. Contrary to popular belief, luminous readers are seldom used by professional mechanics, or by any cheat except the stupid novice. Luminous readers took on a new life, though, when the gaff supply houses developed tinted contact lenses. But, as Mr. Frank Garcia pointed out in *Marked Cards and Loaded Dice*, the contact lenses are not undetectable. They are likely to produce a red tint about the pupil of the eye, especially in profile; and the blink rate of the wearer is likely to be higher than normal. The professional will still avoid luminous readers, but the gaff supply houses will no doubt sell the amateur a great many of these contact lenses at $150 a pair, or more.

At any rate, it is not necessary for the cheat, whoever he may be, to purchase the marked decks. If he has the tinted glasses or visors, he can mark cards before a game by using luminous inks or pencils, or he can mark them during play by using luminous daub.

Nailing. Making an impress in the edge of a card with the thumbnail (or with a special prick) is one of the oldest methods of marking cards during play. In nailing, all the work is done along the edge of the card; but the fingernail or thumbnail, if sharply pointed, can also be used for pegging, in which the work is done on the face of the cards.

Nailing is sometimes called nail-pricking, rim jagging, or punctuation. As Mr. Sidney H. Radner aptly put it in *How to Spot Card Sharps and Their Methods,* indexing could well be another name for nailing; if the work is properly done, the cheat can find a card in the deck much like using a thumb-indexed dictionary.

Pegging. The act of marking cards by means of a thumbtack or special prick (preferably of soft gold, which will make an indentation in the card without puncturing or tearing the surface). Usually, the tack or prick will protrude from a band-aid or tape around the thumb. A sharp thumbnail or fingernail is used for the same purpose, although the indentation will be slightly different. Generally, peg work (also called blistering or punching) is felt with the fingers or thumb rather than read with the eye; hence, it is a convenient method of marking cards for second dealing.

Waving. The act of marking cards in play by bending the key cards around a finger. Cards so waved can often be spotted in an opponent's hand, in the deck, or on top of the deck. Also, waved cards are sometimes used as a crimp for controlling the cut. Bending the corners of cards is a common form of waving.

♥ ♥ ♥

The card cheat need not have marked cards and need not be an accomplished number-two man to fleece the majority of occasional poker players. The examples below are by no means conclusive, but they do give an indication of the cheat's resourcefulness:

Shiner. A mirror or mirrorlike device that a crooked dealer uses to read the cards as they come off the deck. Shiners are often put in pipes, on matchboxes, in a stack of chips, and even in the tips of cigarettes. Rings, watches, shiny cigarette cases, ashtrays, etc., are also used, and women dealers have been known to conceal shiners on the underside of their fingernail tips.

Gerolamo Cardano, an Italian scholar, described shiners and other gaffs in *Liber de ludo aleae (Book on Games of Chance),* which was written around 1520.

Crimp. A break in a deck of cards so that a mechanic, his confederate, or even an unsuspecting player will cut, or is likely to cut, to a particular card or group of cards. The crimp is sometimes used to help the mechanic nullify a cut by sleight of hand; but the mechanic has to be very dexterous to make this manipulation in close play, although it is fairly frequent in two- or three-handed games.

A crimp is made by bending or waving a card or cards. A good crimp is difficult to see but is easy to "feel" once one has the hang of it. One of the most effective crimps is a debone, a card or portion of the deck that has been crimped both sideways and endways. A crimp, especially one that is visible, is sometimes called a bridge.

Holdout Device. A device or technique for taking cards out of the game or putting them back into the game. Many of these devices are quite elaborate and expensive. A chest holdout, for instance, is strapped around the chest and arm. When the operator takes a deep breath, a little mechanical hand, on tongs, reaches down to the edge of his sleeve. When the breath is exhaled, the hand retracts with the cards. Of course, the mechanical principles of operation vary with different makes.

But there are less elaborate devices that are used to hold out cards. The "bug" is a springclasp holdout that is affixed to the underside of the table by an awl or a suction cup; a "spider" is a similar holdout that is attached to the cheat's coat or vest.

Cross-Lift. A system of cheating in which one confederate gives a signal that he holds a good hand and the other bets or raises. It is also called the whipsaw system, the crooked-honest system, or simply the C-H.

False Cut. The cut is the only protection a player has against a stacked deck. Any method of nullifying a legitimate cut, simulating a cut, or cutting to a stacked portion of the deck can be called a method of false cutting. How a mechanic, his confederate, or an unsuspecting player can cut to a certain portion of the deck was discussed under "Crimp."

The most frequently used false cut requires no skill at all. If a player to the dealer's right cuts the deck and leaves both portions on the table, the crooked dealer merely picks up the top portion and puts the deck back exactly as it was. This simple ruse is usually noticed if the dealer picks up the deck immediately after the cut;

but it often goes unnoticed in a loose game if the dealer lights a cigarette or performs some other action to kill a few seconds.

The other methods of accomplishing a false cut require sleight of hand and must be extremely well performed to go unnoticed. The mechanic will usually create some distraction at the table, or else will use his arm as a shield.

False Shuffle. Any shuffle or simulated shuffle that leaves the entire deck, or a stacked portion of it, in its original order. The most obvious false shuffle is the seemingly clumsy riffle in which a block of cards are left in their original order, usually at the top or bottom of the deck.

There are several kinds of overhand false shuffle. (The overhand shuffle is performed by "shuffling" the cards from one hand to the other without using the riffle.) To describe these manipulations would require many pages and a special vocabulary; for a sampling of this kind of jargon, see the quotation from S. W. Erdnase under "Run Up a Hand." One of the more common false shuffles, however, is not an overhand shuffle but is a riffle-type shuffle called the pull-through.

The pull-through looks like an ordinary riffle shuffle. The cards are cut into two packets. Each packet is sprung, and each end is meshed into the other. When the end-meshed cards are pushed together for the block, at a slight angle, the mechanic pulls one packet through the other. As he pulls them through, he seems to halve the deck for another riffle. After the last riffle, though, he is in a bind. He must slap one packet on top of the other, and he can be spotted here unless his hand is quicker than the eye.

Cold Deck. A prestacked deck that is slipped into play is called a cold deck. Cards in play are warmed by friction and by being held in the hand; the cold deck, then, is sometimes perceptively cooler when it is run into the game.

The cold deck can be run into play by the cheat himself or by his accomplice, who may be another player, a kibitzer, or (often) a waiter, bellhop, or someone bringing sandwiches and drinks to the game. A drink spilled on the table, or some other such distraction, usually helps cover the switch, so that the worldly poker player can sometimes spot a cold-decking crew at work even before the stacked cards are run in!

If the prestacked deck is run in after the cut, the cheat has no problem except of not getting caught. But if the deck has to be shuffled or cut, or both, a card mechanic is required. He will have to false shuffle and nullify the cut by one ruse or another. Usually, though, a skilled mechanic won't have to cold-deck his pigeons, and he leaves this blatant form of cheating to crooks with less skill and more gall.

I know of one house game in the South in which a cold deck was run in during the cut. There were seven players. High-Low Draw. The cold deck turned out to be quite hot! Two of the players held pat full houses; two held pat six-lows; and two held fairly good low hands along with flushes. The cheat himself held a draw at a wheel straight flush. He caught it on the draw, of course, and swung both high and low. The pot wasn't as big as might be expected, however, because many of the players were skeptical of the betting and raising. They were a good deal more than merely skeptical after six players held pat!

The glances from player to player and the shaking of heads and such comments as, "That deck sure did get cold!" mounted collectively until one player made a direct accusation. The cheat acted as though he didn't know what a cold deck was. Finally, the houseman, seeing that he was about to lose six good customers, said to the cheat, "We're going to search you. Have you got another deck of cards in your pocket?"

"Hell, I've got three decks in my pocket," the cheat said.

In the end the players got their money back, and the cheat left unharmed. He was shot several weeks later for cheating—but, unfortunately, he wasn't killed. He's still around, and maybe he has learned not to be so foolish as to try to break every player at the table in one hand!

Spread. The spread—a method of cheating in which the cheat must have a confederate and a set of signals—is best explained by example. Say the cheat holds a diamond fourflush. He asks his confederate, by signal, whether he has a diamond. If the confederate does have one, the cheat proceeds to get rid of his off-suit card by palming it onto the discards (no doubt while pretending to push the discards to one side) or by copping it with a holdout device. His confederate, meanwhile, will be palming the diamond in his own hand with its face to his skin. At the showdown, the cheat says, "Flush!" He slaps his cards—only four—onto the table face up but in a packet, so that only the top diamond shows. Quickly saying something like, "Seeing is believing," the confederate reaches out to spread the cards. During this move he deposits the palmed fifth diamond onto the poker hand. During his confederate's move, the cheat will probably be reaching dramatically for the pot to help distract attention from the spread.

Although the spread is usually worked with flushes, it can be used to fill a straight or a full house. Watch for it.

Run Up a Hand. To stack a deck during play, often by arranging discards, is called running up a hand. There are several procedures for running up a hand by using either the overhand shuffle or the riffle shuffle. A description of these methods would probably be unreadable. Consider the following procedure, for running up only two cards, from S. W. Erdnase's classic, *The Expert at the Card Table:*

"The two desired cards are placed on top, under-cut about half the deck, in-jog top card, run two less than twice the number of players, out-jog and shuffle off. Under-cut to out-jog, forming break at in-jog; run one less than number of players, throw to break, run number of players, in-jog and shuffle off. Under-cut to in-jog and throw on top. This action places the two desired cards so that they will fall to the dealer in the first two rounds."

The point here, however, is not to provide a how-to text on running up hands, but to warn the reader of such practice. Any player who toys with the discards or uses the overhand shuffle should be viewed with suspicion.

♥ ♥ ♥

One way to protect yourself against cheats is to see that the cards are cut properly. During World War II, Mr. John Scarne perfected a cut to combat crooked gambling in the armed forces, and card detective Frank Garcia came up with the following variation in his *Marked Cards and Loaded Dice:*

"1. From the middle of the pack, extract two separate packets and put them in a separate pile, one atop the other.

"2. Place the remainder of the deck atop this pile.

"3. Now cut the deck again.

"This procedure will take somewhat longer than a conventional cut, and the other players (especially the stacker!) will cluck impatiently. Let them! Be a turtle! The Garcia cut hopelessly strews any stack all through the deck, and what you lose in time you will save in money."

♥ ♥ ♥

What can be done when you catch a cheat? Nothing, legally. You can't often prove anything in court. Moreover, if you "take the law into your own hands" you may end up in court yourself on some sort of assault charge—or you could even get yourself shot if the cheat feels cornered. So, a more level-headed approach is desirable.

If a professional cheat like a number-two man worms his way into a social game, he'll usually leave if you let him know that you suspect him. I once "detected" a mechanic in a private game whose seconds looked good but sounded almost as though he were dealing sheets of sandpaper. Actually, I suspected the guy the first night I saw him. There was just something about him. . . . But he didn't try anything fancy that first night. Nor the second. But on the third night he brought his buddy. He called Five-Card Stud on one of his deals. His dealing went along smoothly—then a swishing sound started. His accomplice caught a king up, and he dealt himself an ace. When the ace fell, he smiled and said, "Well, what-da-ya-know?"

"It *looked* pretty good," I said.

Quickly the guy cut his eyes my way. He knew that I suspected him. On my next deal, I let the light glare off the top of a few of the cards. The aces and kings had a slight diagonal impress in the left corners, apparently made with the thumbnail. I asked for a new deck. Then the mechanic knew for sure that I was on to him. Neither he nor his buddy ever came back. Yet, I hadn't accused him of anything, and only one of the other regular players ever knew what had gone on.

If you detect a cheat in a house game, talk privately to the man who runs the joint. If he's honest, or a good businessman, he'll appreciate your tip. Then if his observations bear out your suspicions, he'll ask the cheat not to come back.

Some house games, however, are run by cheats. Some private games are, too. In this case, I suggest that you do as I did when I caught a group of football players passing cards to each other back when I was a freshman in college. Did I slap a tackle and punch a guard in the nose? No. I stood up, straightened my tie, and said, "Excuse me, gentlemen, but I have an algebra exam in the morning!"

Mathematics—as I have, I hope, made clear—are a good servant to the poker player but a bad master.

—Hubert Phillips, *Profitable Poker*

Part Two

Mathematics of Poker

Figuring the Odds

If you hold 4 diamonds in Jacks, what are your chances of catching a fifth one on the draw? Well, you have seen 5 of the 52 cards, leaving 47 unaccounted for. Of these, 9 are diamonds. Your chances, then, of making the flush are 9 in 47, or about 1 in 5¼. But the correct odds are 4¼ to 1.

The relation between *odds* and *chances* can be clarified somewhat by looking at a problem from a before-and-after standpoint. If your chances of drawing a diamond to a fourflush are 1 in 5¼, the pot should contain at least $5.25 *after* you make a $1 call. If the odds are 4¼ to 1, the pot should contain at least $4.25 *before* you make a $1 call.

Actually, I prefer to deal in probability rather than in odds, simply because it's easier to calculate the probability in complicated situations. The probability that some event will happen (such as catching the fifth diamond) lies somewhere within the range of 0 to 1. If the probability is 0, the event cannot happen. If the probability is 1, the event must happen. Almost all probabilities are neither 0 nor 1, and are conveniently expressed in decimals. In the calculations that follow, as well as in the tables, I usually express the probabilities in thousandths; thus, a probability of 0.125 would mean that the event will occur on the average of 125 times per thousand cases.

The fundamental formula for calculating probability is simply

$$P = \frac{\text{number of favorable cases}}{\text{number of possible cases}}$$

where the number of possible cases equals the total of the favorable cases plus the unfavorable cases. Taking the diamond fourflush for an example,

$$P = \frac{9}{47} = 0.191$$

where 9 is the number of diamonds left (favorable cases) and 47 is the total number of cards left (possible cases).

Another method of arriving at the probability that an event will happen is first to calculate the probability that the event will not happen and then subtract that figure from 1. The probability of making the flush, then, is

$$P = 1 - \left(\frac{38}{47}\right) = 1 - 0.809 = 0.191$$

where 38 is the number of cards that are not diamonds and 47 is the total number of cards.

If you know your probability of making the flush (and assume that it will win), you can figure the return on your money. Example: When the pot contains $5.25 after you make a $1 call, your investment return is $5.25 × 0.191, or exactly $1; in other words you'll break even over the long run. When the pot contains $10 after you make a $1 call, you'll get back a long-term average of $10 × 0.191 = $1.91 for every one dollar you invest. When the pot contains $3 after you make a $1 call, you'll get back a long-term average of $3 × 0.191 = 57¢ for every one dollar you invest.

Although probability figures are easy to use, some poker players may want to know the odds on particular draws and other situations. If so, the following scheme can be used to convert from probability to *approximate* odds:

$$\text{odds} = \left(\frac{1}{P} - 1\right) \text{ to } 1$$

Thus, the approximate odds against filling the diamond fourflush are

$$\left(\frac{1}{0.191} - 1\right) \text{ to } 1, \text{ or about } 4\frac{1}{4} \text{ to } 1$$

This method of approximating the odds is usually close enough, but very low probabilities rounded off to three decimal places (such as 0.003) will sometimes result in large errors on the approximate odds. If in doubt, compute the odds directly by dividing the favorable cases into the unfavorable cases.

By far the easiest way to figure the favorable cases and unfavorable cases and total possible cases in complex situations is by using what the mathematicians call *combinations*. After going through a lot of derivation, my old freshman algebra text came up with the formula

$$C_{(n,r)} = \frac{n!}{r!(n-r)!}$$

where $C_{(n,r)}$ is the number of combinations of n things taken r at the time. (A notation such as 9! is a short way of writing $9 \times 8 \times 7 \times 6 \times 5 \times 4 \times 3 \times 2 \times 1$.) Take an example: How many poker hands are there in a standard deck of cards? $n = 52$, because there are 52 cards in a standard deck. $r = 5$, because a poker hand contains only 5 cards. The total combinations, then, are

$$C = \frac{52!}{5!(52-5)!} = \frac{52!}{5!47!} = \frac{(52 \cdot 51 \cdot 50 \cdot 49 \cdot 48)47!}{5!47!}$$

Notice that 47! divides out of the equation, so that we need write down only $r!$ and the first 5 (r) figures of n:

$$C = \frac{52 \cdot 51 \cdot 50 \cdot 49 \cdot 48}{5!} = 2,598,960$$

Take another example. How many heart flushes (including the straight flushes) are possible in a standard 52-card deck? Well, $n = 13$ because there are 13 hearts in a standard deck; $r = 5$ because a flush is made up of five cards. So,

$$C = \frac{13 \cdot 12 \cdot 11 \cdot 10 \cdot 9}{5!} = 1,287$$

Another example will show how combinations can be used to determine probability. What is the probability of catching a pat flush in draw poker?

$$P = \frac{\text{favorable cases}}{\text{possible cases}}$$

$$= \frac{\dfrac{13 \cdot 12 \cdot 11 \cdot 10 \cdot 9}{5!} + \dfrac{13 \cdot 12 \cdot 11 \cdot 10 \cdot 9}{5!} + \dfrac{13 \cdot 12 \cdot 11 \cdot 10 \cdot 9}{5!} + \dfrac{13 \cdot 12 \cdot 11 \cdot 10 \cdot 9}{5!} - 40}{\dfrac{52 \cdot 51 \cdot 50 \cdot 49 \cdot 48}{5!}}$$

$$= 0.002$$

Why minus 40 in the numerator? Because these are straight flushes. There are 10 possible ranks of straight flush (ace through 5, deuce through 6, trey through 7, and so on up to and including 10 through ace) and four suits for each rank. So, 10 × 4 = 40.

♥ ♥ ♥

A standard mathematical law states that the probability of two or more independent events taking place is the product of the probabilities that each event will happen. This law is useful when you want to calculate your probability not merely of making your hand but of winning the pot. Assume, for example, that you draw to a fourflush against opponents A and B. Opponent A holds triplets. Opponent B holds two pairs. Your probability of winning the pot is the product of the probability of your filling the flush times the probability that A will not make a full house (or four-of-a-kind) times the probability that B will not make a full house. Borrowing some figures from Table III, the equation for winning becomes

$$P = (0.191)\,(1 - 0.104)\,(1 - 0.085) = 0.157$$

where the term $(1 - 0.104)$ is the probability that A will not improve his hand, since the probability of not improving is 1 minus the probability of improving (0.104). The same for the term $(1 - 0.085)$.

This equation, however, is not quite accurate because the events are not entirely independent. But the figure is close enough, in this case, for all practical purposes. A safer law is

The probability that two successive events both take place is equal to the probability of the first event multiplied by that of the second, the latter being computed on the assumption that the first event has already taken place.*

* *Chance, Luck and Statistics,* by Horace C. Levinson, reprinted by permission of Dover Publications, Inc., New York.

Figuring the probability of catching a pair of aces back to back in Five-Card Stud will illustrate the use of this law. The probability of catching the first ace is 4/52. After you catch it, the probability of catching another ace is 3/51. Thus, the probability of catching both is

$$P = \frac{4 \cdot 3}{52 \cdot 51} = 0.0045$$

The same problem can be worked out by using combinations

$$P = \frac{C_{(4,2)}}{C_{(52,2)}} = \frac{\left(\dfrac{4 \cdot 3}{2!}\right)}{\left(\dfrac{52 \cdot 51}{2!}\right)} = 0.0045$$

Note, however, that if you *already had* the first ace, the probability of catching the second one on the next card would be $3/51 = 0.059$.

Serious students of poker will already have noticed that the odds and probability figures vary from book to book. Most of the modern works are close enough for all practical purposes, and the disparities are merely academic. My quarrel is not that there are these minor disparities but that the authors don't give adequate examples of how they computed their figures. Typically, they set forth a few basic laws of probability and then give a simple example, like how to figure the odds against filling a fourflush in Jacks. But the average college graduate cannot apply the probability laws and simple examples to more complex games like Seven-Card Stud. True, some of the writers give tables for Seven-Card Stud, and most of them are accurate enough. But what about a game like Omaha, on which no figures are available in any book? The serious poker player must compute his own odds and probabilities.

Because no one book can possibly cover the mathematics of all the particular poker games, I have decided to include examples of how to calculate probabilities in some of the more complex situations. If you understand the basic principles and follow the examples given below, you can figure the odds for almost any game.

Figuring Flushes. Assuming that you hold three hearts on the first three cards in Seven-Card Stud, what is the probability of your ending up with a flush? If we ignore (for the purpose of calculation) the up-cards around the board, there are 49 cards from which to form combinations. Of these, 10 are hearts, and you have four more cards to come. There are three possibilities of making a flush. First, you can catch two hearts combined with any two of (49 − 10) other cards. Second, you can catch three hearts combined with any one of (49 − 10) other cards. Third, you can catch four hearts. Our probability equation becomes

$$P = \frac{\text{favorable cases}}{\text{total possible cases}}$$

$$= \frac{\text{cases of 2 } \heartsuit\text{'s + cases of 3 } \heartsuit\text{'s + cases of 4 } \heartsuit\text{'s}}{\text{total possible cases}}$$

$$= \frac{\left(\dfrac{10\cdot 9}{2!}\right)\left(\dfrac{39\cdot 38}{2!}\right) + \left(\dfrac{10\cdot 9\cdot 8}{3!}\right) 39 + \left(\dfrac{10\cdot 9\cdot 8\cdot 7}{4!}\right)}{\left(\dfrac{49\cdot 48\cdot 47\cdot 46}{4!}\right)}$$

$$= 0.180$$

The same answer may be arrived at by using the equation $P = 1 - X$, where P is the probability of filling the flush and X is the probability of not filling it. Using combinations,

$$P = 1 - \left(\frac{\left(\dfrac{39\cdot 38\cdot 37\cdot 36}{4!}\right) + \left(\dfrac{39\cdot 38\cdot 37}{3!}\right) 10}{\dfrac{49\cdot 48\cdot 47\cdot 46}{4!}} \right)$$

$$= 0.180$$

In draw poker, three cards in the same suit are sometimes called a monkey flush, perhaps because only a poor player or a monkey would make a two-card draw to the holding in a game like Jacks. The probability of connecting on a two-card draw is easily figured as follows:

$$P = \frac{\left(\dfrac{10 \cdot 9}{2!}\right)}{\left(\dfrac{47 \cdot 46}{2!}\right)} = 0.042$$

The same sort of reasoning can be applied to almost any stud or widow game if you'll adjust the figures according to how many cards you have seen, how many are yet to come, and so on.

Figuring Straights. How many straights are there in a standard 52-card deck? First consider ace-high straights, composed of some combination of tens, jacks, queens, kings, and aces—but the favorable cases formed from these 20 cards must not contain a pair. Consequently, the $C_{(20,5)}$ formula will not work here. The calculation is made by multiplying the 4 aces times the 4 kings times the 4 queens times the 4 jacks times the 4 tens. That this is the correct procedure is shown by the following chart, showing how many ways 4 aces and 4 kings can combine without pairing:

				Total
♦A♦K	♦A♣K	♦A♠K	♦A♥K	4
♣A♦K	♣A♣K	♣A♠K	♣A♥K	4
♠A♦K	♠A♣K	♠A♠K	♠A♥K	4
♥A♦K	♥A♣K	♥A♠K	♥A♥K	4
total 4 +	4 +	4 +	4 =	16

Then these 16 combinations can further combine with 4 queens, giving 16×4 combinations that do not contain a pair. Then with 4 jacks, giving $16 \times 4 \times 4$. Then with 4 tens, giving $16 \times 4 \times 4 \times 4$, which equals 1,024 ace-high straights.

There are the same number of king-high straights, queen-high straights, and so on down to five-high straights. The total number of straights, then, is $10 \times 1,024 = 10,240$. But 40 of these will be straight flushes, so our total number of regular straights becomes $10,240 - 40 = 10,200$.

The probability of catching a pat straight on the first five cards is

$$P = \frac{10,200}{2,598,960} = 0.004$$

What are your chances of making a straight in Seven-Card Stud if you hold, say, 3-4-5 on the first three cards? Well, the favorable cases *must* include combinations containing A-2, 2-6, or 6-7. Since there are four cards to come, any four-card combination containing A-2, 2-6, or 6-7 would fill the straight. These 16 key cards can make favorable combinations not only with the 33 other cards $(49 - 16 = 33)$ but also with each other. If we let X stand for any of these remaining 33 cards, the favorable cases would comprise combinations of

A-2-X-X	A-A-2-X	A-A-A-2	A-2-2-X	A-2-2-2	A-A-2-2
2-6-X-X	2-2-6-X	2-2-2-6	2-6-6-X	2-6-6-6	2-2-6-6
6-7-X-X	6-6-7-X	6-6-6-7	6-7-7-X	6-7-7-7	6-6-7-7

Notice that all these possibilities are made up of properly matched key cards and X cards. In other words, the first line contains only cards of the A-2 rank and X cards, and so on for the second and third lines. For identification, let's call all these possibilities Set I.

Set II contains any possible arrangement of an X card with key cards of intermixed rank except pairs of key cards:

A-2-6-X	A-2-7-X	2-6-7-X	7-6-A-X

The third set contains possibilities made up of key cards intermixed from rank to rank but excluding the possibilities made up within each rank (which were accounted for in Set. I):

A-A-2-6	A-A-2-7	A-2-6-6	A-2-6-7	A-2-7-7	A-2-2-6
A-2-2-7	2-6-6-7	2-2-6-7	2-6-7-7	6-7-7-A	6-6-7-A
6-7-A-A					

If we group some of our similar cases together, our favorable cases are

$$I = 3 \left[4 \cdot 4 \left(\frac{33 \cdot 32}{2!} \right) + 2 \left(\frac{4 \cdot 3}{2!} \right) 4 \cdot 33 + \right.$$
$$\left. 2 \left(\frac{4 \cdot 3 \cdot 2}{3!} \right) 4 + \left(\frac{4 \cdot 3}{2!} \right) \left(\frac{4 \cdot 3}{2!} \right) \right]$$

$$II = 4 \, (4 \cdot 4 \cdot 4 \cdot 33)$$

$$III = \left[\left(\frac{4 \cdot 3}{2!} \right) 4 \cdot 4 \right] 12 + (4 \cdot 4 \cdot 4 \cdot 4)$$

After all the arithmetic is done, the favorable cases come to 40,156.
The probability of making the straight with the next four cards is
40,156 divided by the possible cases, (49 × 48 × 47 × 46) / 4!. The
answer is 0.190. Any questions?

Actually, most of the calculations of this sort are not quite so
complicated. With only three cards to come and you hold 2-3-4-5,
the favorable cases are reduced to A-X-X, 6-X-X, A-6-X, A-A-6,
6-6-A, A-A-A, and 6-6-6. It's even easier, since you *must* catch either
an ace or a six to fill the straight, to figure the probability of not
catching either an ace or a six and then subtract this figure from one:

$$P = 1 - \left[\frac{\left(\dfrac{40 \cdot 39 \cdot 38}{3!} \right)}{\left(\dfrac{48 \cdot 47 \cdot 46}{3!} \right)} \right] = 0.429$$

Figuring Low Hands. How many wheels are there in a standard
52-card deck? Well, there are 20 cards (four aces, four deuces, four
treys, four 4's, and four 5's) that can contribute to a perfect wheel
low (in the California scale). But they must not pair with each other,
so our equation is the same as for figuring straights, except that
we don't have to subtract the straight flushes. The numbers are
4 × 4 × 4 × 4 × 4 = 1,024.

How many six-low hands? Any 5 of 24 cards can combine as long
as they don't pair. Here, however, we're dealing with 6 ranks of cards
taken 5 at the time. So, a modified (or finagled) combinations
formula can be used:

$$C = \frac{24(23 - 3)\,(22 - 6)\,(21 - 9)\,(20 - 12)}{5!} = 6,144$$

where the term (23 − 3) accounts for the three cards that would pair
the first card, the term (22 − 6) accounts for the six cards that would
pair the first two cards, and so on. But this method gives us the number of hands that are six-low *or lower*. To get the exact number of
six-low hands, we have to subtract the number of wheels, which would
result in 6,144 − 1,024 = 5,120.

If you start off with A-2-3 in Seven-Card Stud High-Low, what is
the probability that you will end up with a six-low or better?

$$P = \frac{\left(\frac{12 \cdot 11}{2!} - 18\right)\left(\frac{37 \cdot 36}{2!}\right) + \left(\frac{12 \cdot 11 \cdot 10}{3!} - 12\right)37 + \left(\frac{12 \cdot 11 \cdot 10 \cdot 9}{4!} - 3\right)}{\frac{49 \cdot 48 \cdot 47 \cdot 46}{4!}}$$

$$= 0.190$$

In the first set of favorable cases, (12×11)/2! gives the number of ways that four 4's, four 5's, and four 6's can combine if taken two at the time. (The 4's, 5's and 6's are the cards that help the six low if you start with A-2-3.) The minus 18 represents the number of pairs in the (12×11)/2! combinations. The 37 is the number of cards left in the deck that do not help the six low (52 minus 3 minus 12), and (37×36)/2! is the number of two-card combinations that do not help the six low—except to combine into four-card combinations with the two-card combinations that do help.

In the second set of favorable cases, the figures show the four-card combinations made up of three-card combinations of the 12 cards that work in the six low (minus 12 sets of triplets) combined with the other 37 cards.

In the third set of favorable cases, the figures show the number of four-card combinations made up from the 12 cards that help the six low, minus 3 sets of triplets.

Remember, however, that the figures in the examples above are valid only for California Lowball. If you play aces high, or straights and flushes high, or with the bug, you'll have to make adjustments in your calculations.

Figuring the Probability of Improving Pairs and Triplets. I have restricted the examples of improving pairs and triplets to simple cases like Jacks. The same principles are easy enough to apply to Seven-Card Stud and other complicated games, but the calculations sometimes become unwieldy. I have included here only straight probability examples. Such special problems as holding a kicker are covered in Part One and under particular games in Part Three.

If you hold A-A-2-3-4 in Jacks, what is your probability of making two pairs on a three-card draw? First of all, there are 47 cards that you haven't seen. The possible cases for your draw are $C_{(47,3)}$.

The favorable cases are a tad more difficult, and are best separated into two sets. In the first set, pairs of deuces, treys, or fours (cards you have seen) can combine with (47 minus 5) other cards, where the minus 5 represents two aces and three cards from any of the ranks. Since there are three ranks and three cards in each rank, the first set of favorable cases is simply $(3 \times 2)/2! \times 3 \times 42$. To these cases must be added the combinations of pairs and kickers made up of the cards you have not seen. There are four 5's, four 6's, and so on up to four kings—a total of 9 ranks. Each rank can form $(4 \times 3)/2!$ pairs. These pairs can combine with (47 minus 6) other cards, where the minus 6 represents two aces and four cards from any of the nine ranks. Putting all this together, our equation becomes

$$P = \frac{\left(\dfrac{3 \cdot 2}{2!}\right) 3 \cdot 42 + \left(\dfrac{4 \cdot 3}{2!}\right) 9 \cdot 41}{\left(\dfrac{47 \cdot 46 \cdot 45}{3!}\right)} = 0.160$$

for making two pairs. But this figure is not for two pairs *or better*. You could end up with triplets, a full house, or even four-of-a-kind, but these are separate calculations.

What are your chances of making triplets? Either of the two aces can combine with any combination of (47 minus 2) other cards—excluding pairs, since catching an ace and a pair would make a full house. As shown in the previous calculation, there are 9 possible pairs made up from the remaining deuces, treys, and fours, and there are 54 possible pairs made up from 9 other ranks of card. Putting all this together, our equation becomes

$$P = \frac{2\left(\dfrac{45 \cdot 44}{2!}\right) - 9 - 54}{\left(\dfrac{47 \cdot 46 \cdot 45}{3!}\right)} = 0.114$$

What are your chances of making a full house? Either of the two aces can combine with $(9 + 54)$ other pairs to give aces full. It's possible, however, to catch another set of triplets to go with your pair of aces. Since you have seen a deuce, a trey, and a 4, there are only 3 sets of triplets that can be made of these ranks of card. From the other 9 ranks, there are $(4 \times 3 \times 2)/3! \times 9$ sets of triplets. Our equation for filling up then becomes

$$P = \frac{2(9 + 54) + 3 + 9\left(\dfrac{4 \cdot 3 \cdot 2}{3!}\right)}{\left(\dfrac{47 \cdot 46 \cdot 45}{3!}\right)} = 0.010$$

What is your probability of making four-of-a-kind? It's slim—but easy to figure. There's only one pair of aces left, and it can combine with any of the other 45 cards. So,

$$P = \frac{1 \cdot 45}{\left(\dfrac{47 \cdot 46 \cdot 45}{3!}\right)} = 0.003$$

What is your probability of making *any* improvement? It's the sum of the probabilities for making the various hands, but remember that the figures are rounded off to the nearest thousandth, so that it's possible for a significant error to accumulate when the figures are added. Here's a sample table:

Hand	Probability
Two pairs	0.160
Triplets	0.114
Full house	0.010
Four-of-a-kind	0.003
Any improvement	0.287

And of course you can figure your chances of making triplets or better (or a full house or better) by simple addition. Here's a table for triplets or better:

Triplets	0.114
Full house	0.010
Four-of-a-kind	0.003
Triplets or *better*	0.127

♥   ♥   ♥

I once settled a bet about the average two-pair hand. Player A bet player B that eights-over is the average, or medial, two-pair hand, based on the following scheme:

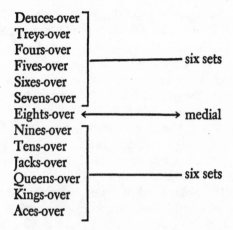

Deuces-over ⎤
Treys-over
Fours-over
Fives-over ├──────── six sets
Sixes-over
Sevens-over ⎦
Eights-over ←──────→ medial
Nines-over ⎤
Tens-over
Jacks-over
Queens-over ├──────── six sets
Kings-over
Aces-over ⎦

Player B, however, maintained that the average two-pair hand is nines-over, simply because deuces can't pair with anything lower.

They both lost! It's jacks-over. Player B was on the right track, but he didn't follow it far enough. As he pointed out, deuces can't pair with anything *lower*. Treys can pair only with deuces. Fours can pair with both treys and deuces. At the other end of the scale, aces can pair with kings, queens, jacks, and so on all the way down to deuces. Obviously, there are more possible two-pair hands with aces-over than with any other two-pair holding.

To arrive at jacks-over as the medial two-pair hand requires a little computation. There are 42 categories of two-pair hands. Of these, 12 are aces-over, simply because aces can pair with 12 lower pairs (kings, queens, jacks . . . deuces). There are 11 combinations of kings-over, because kings can pair with 11 lower pairs. There are 10 combinations of queens-over, because queens can pair with 10 lower pairs. There are 9 combinations of jacks-over, because jacks can pair with 9 lower pairs. Adding up the possible categories of aces-over, kings-over, queens-over, and jacks-over, we get: 12 + 11 + 10 + 9 = 42, which is a little better than half the possible categories of two-pair hands. Thus, jacks-over is the medial two-pair hand.

Another approach would be to figure out the total number of specific two-pair hands—which would be exactly 123,552. To begin with, consider how many ways a pair of aces can be made. Using combinations, the equation would be $(4 \times 3)/2! = 6$. This number can be verified by counting the possibilities: (1) ♠A + ♣A, (2) ♠A + ♥A, (3) ♠A + ♦A, (4) ♣A + ♥A, (5) ♣A + ♦A, and (6) ♥A + ♦A.

So, aces can pair 6 ways, kings can pair 6 ways, and so on for each of the 13 ranks of card. There are, then, $13 \times 6 = 78$ possible pairs. Moreover, any pair may be combined with $78 - 6 = 72$ other pairs. Thus, the total number of two-pair combinations would be $(78 \times 72)/2! = 2,808$. But a *poker* hand comprises five cards, so the two-pair combinations could have any off-card as a kicker. There would be $11 \times 4 = 44$ off-cards. So, the total number of two-pair poker hands would be $2,808 \times 44 = 123,552$.

To find the medial two-pair hand, we must calculate the number of hands that can be made with aces-over, kings-over, and so on. For aces-over, 6 pairs of aces can combine with $12 \times 6 = 72$ other pairs and 44 off-cards. The total number of aces-over hands is therefore $6 \times 72 \times 44 = 19,008$.

The total number of kings-over hands would be less and could be figured as follows: 6 pairs of kings can combine with $11 \times 6 = 66$ lower pairs and 44 off-cards. The total number of kings-over hands would then be $6 \times 66 \times 44 = 17,424$.

The same sort of mathematical reasoning would work all the way down to the end of the scale, and the following table would result:

Hand	Number
Aces-over	19,008
Kings-over	17,424
Queens-over	15,840
Jacks-over	14,256
Tens-over	12,672
Nines-over	11,088
Eights-over	9,504
Sevens-over	7,920
Sixes-over	6,336
Fives-over	4,752
Fours-over	3,168
Treys-over	1,584
Deuces-over	0
total	123,552

If we add up the possible two-pair hands that can be made of either aces-over, kings-over, queens-over, or jacks-over, we get:

Aces-over	19,008
Kings-over	17,424
Queens-over	15,840
Jacks-over	14,256
total	66,528

Again, this figure is a little more than half the possible 123,552 two-pair hands.

The fact that jacks-over, not eights-over or nines-over, is the average two-pair hand has an important bearing on how strongly a particular two-pair holding should be played. This bit of oddsmanship is especially useful when you hold two-pairs and suspect your opponent of also holding two-pairs; if you hold jacks-over, you have about a 50–50 chance of winning (*if* you have correctly assessed your opponent's holding); if, on the other hand, you hold sevens-over, you should call the bet only if the pot contains quite a bit more than what it costs you. The exact odds could be obtained for specific hands, but to cover every possible situation would require enough tabular matter to exhaust the typesetter's patience. Just remember that you don't usually have the best of a two-pair showdown if you hold anything lower than jacks-over.

It has been said that the play of two pairs in Jacks or Guts will determine whether one comes out winner or loser over the long haul. Well, merely knowing the correct figures on the medial two-pair hand will not of itself make you an expert two-pairsman, but it will help you win a little more—or lose a little less.

♥ ♥ ♥

How valid are the purely mathematical probabilities in real poker? They're pretty close. Once I calculated a set of odds on a poker game that was new to me. Then I sat down and dealt out a thousand hands, tabulating the results as I went. According to the calculations, the probability of making a flush, for example, was 0.065. The actual figure was 0.069. The difference was four flushes per thousand deals. That's pretty close.

I do think, however, that the figures tend to run higher in real

poker than in the calculations. Players are constantly grouping pairs
and suits together in their hands. Shuffles are seldom thorough. If a
player throws in a pair of aces in Jacks, there is a good chance that the
mel will survive a poor shuffle. Then if the mel ends up in the bottom
half of the deck after the cut, there is a good chance that some player
around the table will catch the cards on the draw.

Even a thorough shuffle, after the cards have been grouped, does
not leave the distribution on an entirely random basis. Consider a
perfect shuffle in a four-handed game. A pair of aces are thrown in
together. The dealer makes a perfect shuffle, so that a queen (or some
card) falls between the two aces. On the next shuffle, a deuce falls in
between the first ace and the queen, and a trey falls in between the
queen and the second ace. If this mel ends up near the top after the
cut, one of the players around the board will catch the pair of aces.
Moreover, the shuffles need not be perfect for this to happen. On the
first shuffle, the aces could remain together, then be separated by a
bloc of three cards on the next shuffle.

Anyhow, this sort of thing happens far too often to be attributed to
random distribution. The complete poker player, then, will adjust his
game somewhat as the session progresses and the shuffle becomes less
and less thorough.

Another question that has a bearing on the validity of the mathematical probabilities is whether or not cards "run." Yes, they do—
but this in no way contradicts probability. Indeed, it would be most
unusual, according to the theory of large numbers, if a poker player
didn't catch a hot or cold run of cards from time to time. The mistake
that most gamblers make is thinking that their luck must change.
Having caught a thousand poor poker hands, however, in no way in-
fluences the chances on the next deal. The odds remain the same, no
matter what has gone before. A deck of cards has no memory—and
certainly no conscience or partiality. As a wise old stud player once
told me, "The cards can run bad all night and then get worse'n hell
just before daylight!" They can run good all night, too. So . . . limit
your losses but let your winnings mount.

Mathematical Tables

TABLE I
POSSIBLE POKER HANDS

Hand	Standard Deck		With Joker		With Bug		Deuces Wild	
	Number	Prob*	Number	Prob*	Number	Prob*	Number	Prob*
Five-of-a-kind	—	–	13	0.000	1	0.000	672	0.000
Straight flush	40	0.000	204	0.000	204	0.000	4,556	0.002
Four-of-a-kind	624	0.000	3,120	0.001	828	0.000	30,816	0.012
Full house	3,744	0.001	6,552	0.002	4,368	0.002	12,672	0.005
Flush	5,108	0.002	7,804	0.003	7,804	0.003	13,204	0.005
Straight	10,200	0.004	20,532	0.007	20,532	0.007	66,236	0.026
Triplets	54,912	0.021	137,280	0.048	63,480	0.022	355,056	0.139
Two pairs	123,552	0.048	123,552	0.043	138,600	0.048	95,040	0.038
One pair	1,098,240	0.423	1,268,088	0.442	1,154,560	0.402	1,222,048	0.478
No pair	1,302,540	0.501	1,302,540	0.454	1,479,308	0.515	798,660	0.312
Totals:	2,598,960		2,869,685		2,869,685		2,598,960	

* Probability of catching on first five cards. The figures are rounded off to thousandths; for example, the probability of catching four-of-a-kind on the first five cards with a standard deck is 0.000244, but this becomes 0.000 when rounded off to the nearest thousandth.

TABLE II
POSSIBLE LOW HANDS

Hand	California Lowball		Sixty-four		Seventy-five	
	Number	Prob *	Number	Prob *	Number	Prob *
Wheel	1,024	0.000	–	–	–	–
Six	5,120	0.002	4,080	0.002	–	–
Seven	15,384	0.006	14,280	0.006	4,080	0.002
Eight	35,924	0.014	34,680	0.014	14,280	0.006
Nine	71,904	0.028	70,380	0.027	34,680	0.014
Ten	129,528	0.051	127,500	0.050	70,380	0.027
Six or lower	6,144	0.002	4,080	0.002	–	–
Seven or lower	21,528	0.008	18,360	0.007	4,080	0.002
Eight or lower	57,452	0.022	53,040	0.021	18,360	0.007
Nine or lower	129,356	0.051	123,420	0.048	53,040	0.021
Ten or lower	258,884	0.101	250,920	0.098	123,420	0.048

* Probability of catching on first five cards, rounded off to the nearest thousandth.

TABLE III
PROBABILITY OF IMPROVING ON THE DRAW IN JACKS AND SIMILAR GAMES*

You Draw	Hand After the Draw							
	Straight Flush	Fours	Full House	Flush	Straight	Trips	Two Pairs	Any Imp.
One card to:								
Trips & kicker	—	0.021	0.064	—	—	—	—	0.085
Two pairs	—	—	0.085	—	—	—	—	0.085
Straight flush:								
Bobtail	0.043	—	—	0.149	0.128	—	—	0.319
Inside †	0.021	—	—	0.170	0.064	—	—	0.255
Flush	—	—	—	0.191	—	—	—	0.191
Straight:								
Bobtail	—	—	—	—	0.170	—	—	0.170
Inside †	—	—	—	—	0.085	—	—	0.085
Two cards to:								
Trips	—	0.043	0.061	—	—	—	—	0.104
Pair & kicker	—	0.001	0.008	—	—	0.078	0.172	0.260
Flush	—	—	—	0.042	—	—	—	—
Bobtail	—	—	—	—	0.044	—	—	—
Three cards to:								
One pair	—	0.003	0.010	—	—	0.114	0.160	0.287
Flush	—	—	—	0.010	—	—	—	—

* With standard 52-card deck.
† And closed-end straights.

TABLE IV
PROBABILITY IN LOWBALL DRAW*

Cards Drawn	Wheel	Six	Seven	Eight	Nine	Ten	Bust †
Final Hand (or Better) in the California Scale							
One to A-2-3-4	0.085	0.170	0.255	0.340	0.426	0.511	—
Two to A-2-3	0.015	0.044	0.089	0.148	0.222	0.311	—
Final Hand (or Better) in the Sixty-four Scale							
One to A-2-3-4	—	0.085	0.170	0.255	0.340	0.426	0.085
One to ♥A-2-3-4	—	0.064	0.128	0.191	0.255	0.319	0.255
One to 2-3-4-5	—	—	0.085	0.170	0.255	0.340	0.170
One to A-2-3-6	—	0.170	0.255	0.340	0.426	0.511	—
Two to A-2-6	—	0.044	0.089	0.148	0.222	0.311	—
Final Hand (or Better) in the Seventy-five Scale							
One to 2-3-4-5	—	—	0.085	0.170	0.255	0.340	0.085
One to 3-4-5-6	—	—	—	0.085	0.170	0.255	0.170
One to ♥3-4-5-6	—	—	—	0.064	0.128	0.191	0.319
One to 2-3-4-7	—	—	0.170	0.255	0.340	0.426	—
Two to 2-3-7	—	—	0.044	0.089	0.148	0.222	—

* Based on standard 52-card deck.
† On straights and flushes.

TABLE V
SEVEN-CARD STUD WITH 52-CARD DECK

You Hold	Final Hand (but Not "or Better")						
	Fours	Full House	Flush	Straight	Trips	Two Pairs	Any Imp.
Three cards:							
A-A-A	0.082	0.331	–	–	–	–	0.413
A-A-X	0.005	0.075	–	–	0.101	0.430	0.611
8-9-10	–	–	–	0.190	–	–	–
A-K-Q	–	–	–	0.072	–	–	–
♥-♥-♥	–	–	0.180	–	–	–	–
Four cards:							
A-A-A-X	0.062	0.327	–	–	–	–	0.389
A-A-K-K	0.005	0.231	–	–	–	–	0.236
A-A-X-X	0.003	0.053	–	–	0.083*	0.416	0.555
8-9-10-X	–	–	–	0.112	–	–	–
8-9-10-J	–	–	–	0.429	–	–	–
7-8-10-J	–	–	–	0.247	–	–	–
A-K-Q-10	–	–	–	0.234	–	–	–
A-K-Q-X	–	–	–	0.038	–	–	–
♥-♥-♥-♥	–	–	0.472	–	–	–	–
♥-♥-♥-X	–	–	0.106	–	–	–	–
Five cards:							
A-A-A-X-X	0.043	0.291	–	–	–	–	0.333
A-A-K-K-X	0.002	0.166	–	–	–	–	0.167
A-A-X-X-X	0.001	0.025	–	–	0.070	0.375	0.471
8-9-10-X-X	–	–	–	0.044	–	–	–
8-9-10-J-X	–	–	–	0.315	–	–	–
7-8-10-J-X	–	–	–	0.165	–	–	–
A-K-Q-10-X	–	–	–	0.165	–	–	–
♥-♥-♥-♥-X	–	–	0.350	–	–	–	–
♥-♥-♥-X-X	–	–	0.042	–	–	–	–
Six cards:							
A-A-A-X-X-X	0.022	0.196	–	–	–	–	0.217
A-A-K-K-X-X	–	0.087	–	–	–	–	0.087
A-A-K-K-Q-Q	–	0.130	–	–	–	–	0.130
A-A-X-X-X-X	–	–	–	–	0.043	0.261	0.304
8-9-10-J-X-X	–	–	–	0.174	–	–	–
7-8-10-J-X-X	–	–	–	0.087	–	–	–
A-K-Q-10-X-X	–	–	–	0.087	–	–	–
♥-♥-♥-♥-X-X	–	–	0.196	–	–	–	–

* For aces only; any other triplets would make a full house.

TABLE VI
SEVEN-CARD STUD HIGH-LOW WITH 52-CARD DECK

You Hold	Final Low (or Better) on California Scale				Final High Hand		
	Wheel	Six	Seven	Eight	Full House*	Flush †	Straight ‡
Three cards:							
A-2-3	0.072	0.190	0.333	0.483	–	–	0.072
2-3-4	0.072	0.190	0.333	0.483	–	–	0.131
3-4-5	0.072	0.190	0.333	0.483	–	–	0.190
♥A-2-7	0.013	0.047	0.333	0.483	–	0.180	–
A-2-K	0.013	0.047	0.107	0.196	–	–	0.013
A-A-2	0.013	0.047	0.107	0.196	0.080	–	0.013
A-A-A	0.001	0.006	0.018	0.042	0.413	–	0.001
Four cards:							
A-2-3-4	0.234	0.429	0.587	0.713	–	–	0.234
2-3-4-5	0.234	0.429	0.587	0.713	–	–	0.429
♥A-2-6-7	0.004	0.112	0.587	0.713	–	0.472	–
♥A-2-7♦K	0.004	0.015	0.209	0.324	–	0.106	–
A-2-3-K	0.038	0.112	0.209	0.324	–	–	0.038
A-2-K-Q	0.004	0.015	0.037	0.074	–	–	0.004
A-A-2-3	0.038	0.112	0.209	0.324	0.056	–	0.038
A-A-2-2	0.004	0.015	0.037	0.074	0.236	–	0.004
A-A-A-2	0.004	0.015	0.037	0.074	0.389	–	0.004
Five cards:							
A-2-3-4-K	0.165	0.315	0.450	0.570	–	–	0.165
2-3-4-5-K	0.165	0.315	0.450	0.570	–	–	0.315
♥A-2-6-7♦J	–	0.044	0.450	0.570	–	0.350	–
♥A-2-7♦J-Q	–	–	0.089	0.148	–	0.042	–
A-A-2-3-4	0.165	0.315	0.450	0.570	0.026	–	0.165
A-A-2-2-3	0.015	0.044	0.089	0.148	0.167	–	0.015
A-A-A-2-3	0.015	0.044	0.089	0.148	0.334	–	0.015
Six cards:							
A-2-3-4-K-Q	0.087	0.174	0.261	0.348	–	–	0.087
2-3-4-5-K-Q	0.087	0.174	0.261	0.348	–	–	0.174
♥A-2-6-7♦J-Q	–	–	0.261	0.348	–	0.196	–
A-A-A-2-3-4	0.087	0.174	0.261	0.348	0.217	–	0.087

* Or better.
† Including straight flushes.
‡ Not including high straights.

TABLE VII
PROBABILITY OF PAIRING YOUR HOLE CARD* IN FIVE-CARD STUD

	Hole Cards Exposed		
	0	1	2
Three cards to come: Cards Seen			
3	0.176	0.120	0.062
4	0.180	0.122	0.063
5	0.183	0.125	0.064
6	0.187	0.127	0.065
7	0.191	0.130	0.067
8	0.195	0.133	0.068
9	0.199	0.136	0.070
10	0.204	0.139	0.071
Two cards to come: Cards Seen			
5	0.125	0.084	0.043—
6	0.128	0.086	0.043+
7	0.130	0.088	0.044
8	0.133	0.090	0.045
9	0.136	0.092	0.047
10	0.139	0.094	0.048
11	0.143	0.096	0.049
12	0.146	0.099	0.050
One card to come: Cards Seen			
7	0.067	0.044	0.022
8	0.068	0.045	0.023—
9	0.070	0.047	0.023+
10	0.071	0.048	0.024—
11	0.073	0.049	0.024+
12	0.075	0.050	0.025
13	0.077	0.051	0.026—
14	0.079	0.053	0.026+
15	0.081	0.054	0.027

* Or a particular up card.

TABLE VIII
CINCINNATI HIGH-LOW AND SIMILAR WIDOW GAMES

You Hold	Low Hand (or Better) —on California Scale			Final High Hand *			
	Wheel	Six	Seven	Fours	Full House	Flush	Straight Flush
A-2-3-4-10	0.373	0.625	0.788	—	—	—	—
A-2-3-10-J	0.119	0.297	0.485	—	—	—	—
K-K-K-6-9	—	—	—	0.106	0.686	—	—
K-K-Q-Q-J	—	—	—	0.018†	0.373	—	—
A-A-J-7-9	—	—	—	0.009‡	0.194‡	—	—
♦-♦-♦-X	—	—	—	—	—	0.672	—
♦-♦-X-X	—	—	—	—	—	0.285	—
♦ 9-10-J-Q-X	—	—	—	—	—	—	0.204
♦ 8-9-J-Q-X	—	—	—	—	—	—	0.106
♦ 9-10-J-X-X	—	—	—	—	—	—	0.026

* Note: The probabilities listed do not account for pat hands and triplets that turn up in the widow from time to time.
† Only for four kings or four queens.
‡ Only for four aces or aces full.

TABLE IX
HOLD ME AND SIMILAR WIDOW GAMES

| You Hold | | Final Hand (but Not "or Better") | | | | | |
Down	Widow	Full House *	Flush	Straight	Trips	Two Pairs	One Pair †
A-K	—	0.016	—	0.027	0.030	0.149 ‡	0.384
K-K	—	0.072	—	—	0.120	0.359	—
10-J	—	—	—	0.088	—	—	—
♥♥	—	—	0.064	—	—	—	—
A-K	2-7-8	—	—	—	0.006	0.057 ‡	0.228
K-K	K-2-7	0.333	—	—	—	—	—
K-Q	K-Q-2	0.167	—	—	—	—	—
K-K	2-7-8	0.026	—	—	0.070	0.375	—
A-K	K-7-8	0.026	—	—	0.070	0.375	—
10-J	9-Q-2	—	—	0.315	—	—	—
10-J	A-K-2	—	—	0.165	—	—	—
♥♥	♥-♥-X	—	0.350	—	—	—	—
♥♥	♥-X-X	—	0.042	—	—	—	—

Note: The probabilities listed do not account for pat hands and triplets that turn up in the widow from time to time.
* Or better.
† Disregarding communal pairs.
‡ Including one communal pair.

TABLE X
COMBINATIONS OF n THINGS TAKEN r AT THE TIME

n	2	3	4	5	n	2	3	4	5
53	1,378	23,426	292,825	2,869,685	28	378	3,276	20,475	98,280
52	1,326	22,100	270,725	2,598,960	27	351	2,925	17,550	80,730
51	1,275	20,825	249,900	2,349,060	26	325	2,600	14,950	65,780
50	1,225	19,600	230,300	2,118,760	25	300	2,300	12,650	53,130
49	1,176	18,424	211,876	1,906,884	24	276	2,024	10,626	42,504
48	1,128	17,296	194,580	1,712,304	23	253	1,771	8,855	33,649
47	1,081	16,215	178,365	1,533,939	22	231	1,540	7,315	26,334
46	1,035	15,180	163,185	1,370,754	21	210	1,330	5,985	20,349
45	990	14,190	148,995	1,221,759	20	190	1,140	4,845	15,504
44	946	13,244	135,751	1,086,008	19	171	969	3,876	11,628
43	903	12,341	123,410	962,598	18	153	816	3,060	8,568
42	861	11,480	111,930	850,668	17	136	680	2,380	6,188
41	820	10,660	101,270	749,398	16	120	560	1,820	4,368
40	780	9,880	91,390	658,008	15	105	455	1,365	3,003
39	741	9,139	82,251	575,757	14	91	364	1,001	2,002
38	703	8,436	73,815	501,942	13	78	286	715	1,287
37	666	7,770	66,045	435,897	12	66	220	495	792
36	630	7,140	58,905	376,992	11	55	165	330	462
35	595	6,545	52,360	324,632	10	45	120	210	252
34	561	5,984	46,376	278,256	9	36	84	126	126
33	528	5,456	40,920	237,336	8	28	56	70	56
32	496	4,960	35,960	201,376	7	21	35	35	21
31	465	4,495	31,465	169,911	6	15	20	15	6
30	435	4,060	27,405	142,506	5	10	10	5	1
29	406	3,654	23,751	118,755	4	6	4	1	–

The more wild cards and crazy rules, the greater the expert's advantage.

—JOHN R. CRAWFORD

Part Three

Dealer's Choice

The majority of casinos and public poker houses allow only a few standard games to be dealt, and usually only a particular game is played at any one table. But most of the social and private poker sessions from coast to coast are dealer's choice, in which each player has the privilege of choosing the game he wants to deal.

Many games give the dealer a decided advantage. Consequently, a few groups, made up of serious poker players, require that such games, once called, be dealt for a complete round so that everyone has the same advantage on his deal. But most groups don't play this way and never will. In these sessions knowledgeable players can gain a considerable positional advantage simply by choosing their games. All draw poker gives the dealer an advantage—especially the "pass and out" kind. Substitution games, widow games where the man to the dealer's left is always the first to speak, and numbers games like Seven and Twenty-Seven also give the dealer an advantage. The dealer has no advantage in regular stud forms—unless he is quick with the cards.

Although dozens of dealer's choice games are described in the following pages, no one book—and certainly no single writer—could possibly cover every poker game that has ever been thought up. Even if such a list could be obtained, it would be out of date before publication. Still, I believe that the games covered here provide a large enough repertoire to see one through any serious dealer's choice session. If not, the principles of poker in Part One can be adapted to almost any game that can be called poker.

Some writers have attempted to classify the various poker games by families. The terms closed poker (draw) and open poker (stud) are often used, and I've seen and toyed with all sorts of family trees. Any such classification does not hold up, simply because the poker games don't fit. One of the most popular forms of poker today is neither stud nor draw, and has principles that are not common to either one. It's widow poker with communal up cards, such as Cincinnati, Bedsprings, Southern Cross, X-Marks-the-Spot, Hold Me, and others. Then we get into the various stud forms with substitutions. Then option poker like Take It or Leave It. Then Pass the Trash. Then "roll 'em back" games. So, instead of trying to fit the dealer's choice games into some family-tree scheme, I have arranged them alphabetically for ease of reference. The major difficulty with an alphabetical arrangement is that there are no universal names for some of the games. (Even authorities on poker have trouble with nomenclature. One writer, called "the Hoyle of our century," described Anaconda one way in his text and another way in his glossary!) I have, therefore, listed the variant names along with a reference to what I consider to be the most widely accepted names, under which the main text appears.

Where sample hands are specified, X refers to a card that does not figure in the evaluation of the hand (e.g., "2-3-5-X-X" under Bedsprings).

ACEPOTS

This draw game is very similar to Jacks or Better to Open. The only difference is that you must hold a pair of aces or better (instead of jacks or better) before you can open the pot. The higher opening requirement tightens up the playable hands considerably, as compared to Jacks. Obviously, any pair lower than aces become short. Fold anything less than aces or two pairs unless several sweeten antes have fattened up the pot. Play fourflushes and bobtails only if the odds are right, and they seldom will be when the pot is opened on the first go around. If no one has opened for several deals, however, the pot may offer calling odds on short pairs, inside straights, and maybe even monkey flushes.

The mechanics of the deal, basic strategy, and so on are covered in the main draw entry under Jacks. Carding for draw poker was discussed in Chapter 6, and the probabilities for the various hands and draws are listed in Tables I and III in Part Two, pages 108 and 110.

ACEY–DEUCEY

See Hurricane.

ALTERNATE STRAIGHT
See Special Hands.

AMARILLO
See Hold Me.

ANACONDA
The only royal I ever caught, without the aid of wild cards, was on the go in Anaconda. Players who are familiar with the game will know that I had to bust my royal in order to "Pass the Trash," as the game is sometimes called. This traumatic experience nearly turned me forever against Anaconda and all who deal it! Yet, I realize that this seemingly crazy game does in fact give the player who masters it more opportunities than almost any other game to exercise the various poker skills.

On the go, each Anaconda player is dealt seven cards down. He keeps his best four and passes three to his left (in some circles only two trash cards are passed on). After receiving three cards from the player on his right, he sorts out his best five-card poker hand and discards two. Then he arranges the remaining five to roll 'em back—and gets set for a betting interval after each roll. At the showdown, each active player will have four up cards and one hole card, as in Five-Card Stud. To complicate the game further—thereby giving the expert the more advantage—Anaconda is usually played high-low.

Most groups have a betting interval before the trash is passed. Therefore, you must know which four-card combinations, selected from the original seven, are worth playing. The following staying requirements are based on conservative play:

1. Four low cards. Preferably not higher than a 6 (based on California Lowball). If you make a low hand when the trash is passed, evaluate it carefully before involving yourself in the roll 'em back betting intervals. Beware the rough 7.

2. High triplets. Preferably three aces and a low card. Low triplets plus a low kicker are also worth a play, but proceed very carefully if you fill a low or middling full house. Remember that you face four betting intervals and that each player can arrange his hand deceptively for the roll 'em back phase.

3. Two pairs. Play only aces over a small pair. Aces and deuces give you a chance for either high or low, but kings and queens don't. (The trouble with playing aces, however, is that players shooting for low aren't likely to pass you one.) In loose circles, any two pairs are worth a modest call, but remember that in such play several full houses may be contending for high money. Kings and queens make a much better drawing hand than kings and deuces; tripping *either* kings or queens would probably get you half the pot, but tripping deuces may only get you in trouble.

4. Straights and flushes. Play these only incidentally to potential low hands.

5. Straight flushes. Play four cards to a bobtail straight flush only in family pots. You don't have a good gamble, from a strictly mathematical viewpoint, against only two or three active players. On the other hand, if you do hit you're almost certain to win high money—and may even swing both ways against those full houses.

♥ ♥ ♥

Problem hands occur from time to time in Anaconda, and you'll have to make decisions on whether to play high or low. As a rule, go for low. One of the toughest decisions in Anaconda is when you hold A-A-A-2-3-4-K. Do you keep A-2-3-4, in which case four cards (the 5's) would make you a wheel and eight cards (the 5's plus the 6's) would make you a sixty-four or better? Or do you keep A-A-A-K, in which case four cards (three K's plus an A) would make you aces full of kings or better, not counting the possible pairs that may be passed your way? Or do you hold A-A-A-2, which still has a chance of making a low hand?

In cards speak, I would hold A-2-3-4. A wheel, if it connects, would make a cinch low hand and could win high as well. In chips declare or consecutive declaration, I would hold A-A-A-2 if I thought that several active opponents would survive the trash, but I would go low in a tight game against only one or two active opponents. As shown in Chapter 7, it is seldom advisable to play high against only one or two players. But I feel that playing low categorically is a mistake in Anaconda.

Whether you should play border or decision hands high or low depends in part on what sort of player is passing the trash to you.

If he is a player who always shoots for low, then he isn't likely to pass many wheel cards your way. Also, what cards you play—as well as how far and which way—depends on the number of players in the game; if you're sitting in a seven-handed game (where 49 of the 52 cards will be out) and most of the players see all bets to the bitter end, you'll need a hand that figures to win over the long haul. It doesn't make too much difference whether it's a very good low hand or a very good high hand *if* most of the players stay in all the way. In such play, hand in and hand out, it takes a full house for high and a six for low. Fold any worse hand, except possibly a seventy-four or an ace-high flush that also makes a middling low hand, such as ♣A-2-4-7-8. Although Anaconda gives one a good deal of room for bluffery and strategy, it is best to sit tight in very loose play until you make a solid hand. Fancy footwork during the roll 'em back phase will just get you in trouble.

In more conservative play, however, you may want to chip along on a mediocre hand until you see which way the opposition is going. Against two or three opponents, you can sometimes determine that you have a cinch low on a rough eight when the second roll card is up. But if the betting gets rambunctious, or if it looks like you'll have competition, get out fast.

In competent play, your betting, bluffery, and roll 'em back strategy should sometimes be geared to drive players out, especially in cards speak. If for example you end up with A-A-A-2-2, you will want to roll first a deuce and then an ace, which look mighty low. Bet heavily. If you succeed in driving out the low hands, you may win *all* the pot because you've got the highest and lowest full house! Your alternative here would be to sandbag, keeping in as many players as possible. But in really conservative play, you may not have more than two active opponents anyway, in which case it's best to beat one of them both ways instead of getting half of what one of two opponents put into the pot. If one player calls $10 and you beat him both ways, you win $10. If two players call $10 and you have to split the pot with one or the other of them, you will net only $5.

How you roll 'em back is sometimes very important. Not long ago I saw a player roll two aces on the first two cards. Immediately I figured that he had spiked a low hand and was trying to back in for high, and I was right. He turned up the two aces and bet heavily to drive out the high players. If he had held aces full, or even four aces, he wouldn't have had to expose a pair until the third roll. He would have shown Q-A-Q-A/(A) if he had aces full of queens (or maybe A-Q-A-Q). I held a seven-high straight and raised his bet, showing 4-5. He folded two rolls and two bets later when I showed 3-4-5-6 and he showed A-A-5-2. My opponent for low showed 2-3-4-5, and had a 6 down. So, I won high on a hand that I would have folded if the bluffer had exposed his second ace on the third roll; in fact, I might have folded if his second roll had been a high card. He would have shown A-Q or Q-A, which has got to be a high hand. My opponent for low would have shown 2-3, and I probably wouldn't have bucked him with the roughest 7 in the deck. This is a good example of a play in which the strategist failed to consider his opponent's analysis. So, if you're going to try this sort of footwork in Anaconda and other roll 'em back games, make your bluff on the third roll, not the second, unless you're playing oneupmanship with another strategist!

♥ ♥ ♥

Don't forget to remember which cards you passed, and which cards were passed to you. This can be important. If you hold the two black deuces and catch a red one, be sure that the red one shows on the roll back, unless you want the player to the right to know your hole card! For example, you hold 10's full of queens. You roll 10-Q-10-Q/(10) and the man on your right has J-9-J-9/(J). If he passed you the ♦ 10 and you leave it down, he will know that his jacks full beats you; if you had turned it up and kept another 10 down, he wouldn't know whether you had 10's full or queens full.

Sometimes you will want the man on your right to think he knows one of your cards. For example, you hold A-2-3-4, and he passes you a 5, a K, and the ♣2. You throw away the king and the ♣2, then expose your original deuce on the first or second roll. (Your best roll here would probably be A-2.) If your opponent remembered that he passed you the ♣2, he may figure you for aces full. If so, he may stick around for a few bets on a mediocre low hand—or he may even fold a full house high hand, which would of course increase your chances of swinging with your Little Minnie.

I admit that I have been making fine points here, but I want to emphasize that they are only examples of many other fine points that, when summed up, give the expert such an advantage in Anaconda.

BASEBALL

In his book *Fortune Poker*, George Coffin said, "That great All-American Poker game is Baseball! It is Seven-Card Stud with all nines (innings) and treys (three strikes) wild. Whenever a player is served a four showing (four balls), [the] dealer immediately gives him an extra free hole card (free base). In the original version of the game, all treys were strictly hand-fouling cards. The moment you got a trey up, you had three strikes and you were out of the game. In the popular modern version, the trey is another wild card with penalty attached. It does not knock a player out, for he has the privilege of buying his way back into the game by paying into the pot its equal value. It is advisable to limit this penalty to 20 chips lest the game get too rough.

"There is little point in staying on the first three cards without a high pair, a wild card, or three cards of a straight flush. And if the fifth card fails to give you at least three aces or any four cards to a straight flush, you should drop. Four-of-a-kind make a common hand in the end. Only straight flushes and five-of-a-kind have class. For this reason, don't pay a big forfeit for a trey with less than four cards to a straight flush or four-of-a-kind toward the end."

My objection to Baseball is that, once started, it tends to dominate the play because even in low-limit poker the pots can mount up out of all proportion to conservative games like Jacks. A case in point. I sometimes play in a 25¢ limit game in which Baseball is dealt. The players felt that if they had to match the pot on treys, they should be able to bet the same amount to protect their hand. Then they started matching and betting the pot on 9's as well as on treys. I have seen pots in this session that held well over $50! After winning —or losing—such a pot, a player isn't interested in reverting to a tamer game with two-bit limits. This group would have a better, more well-rounded session if they would take Coffin's advice and limit the penalty on wild cards. Two bucks (in quarter limit) would be steep enough.

The playing requirements that Coffin recommended are all right for fairly loose play. But if there is no penalty limit, these requirements should be tightened considerably. Frankly, I don't want to become involved in a no-ceiling Baseball game unless I have at least two wild cards on the go, or maybe a wild card and two natural aces. Why so tight? It's a matter of mathematics. Let the pot contain $20. You match $20 with a trey up. Then you bet $20. In all, you are sending $40 after the original $20. If anybody calls your bet, they are sending only $20 after $60.

An even worse situation—and better calling situation—takes shape in Baseball games where you have to match the pot on treys but can bet only a fixed amount. In a very loose 25¢ limit game, the pot can easily amount to $10. You catch a trey, match the pot, and bet the limit—thereby sending $10.25 after $10. Your opponents can then send a mere two-bits after $20.25, and of course they'll be in there drawing to those straight flushes. So . . . don't match those big pots unless you're really loaded.

BASEBALL HIGH–LOW

Deal this dilly exactly like Baseball for high, but get set for some tougher decisions. Often you'll find yourself with a good high hand along with a perfect low. Beware of swinging in chips declare or consecutive declaration because too many wheels are filled in this game. It's not uncommon to see two or three perfect lows tangle in one pot. So, if you end up with five aces and a wheel, settle for high money if two or three hands around the board look even halfway low. Beware of even a single 4 showing; it fits a perfect low and also gives your opponent an extra down card, so that a sorry looking hand like (?-?-?)/4-K-Q-J/(?) can turn out to be very low.

Baseball is the only high-low game in which I prefer to play the sixty-four low instead of the wheel. The reason is that a 5-spot is a dangerous card in sixty-four, and most players don't know just how dangerous. A 5 seems like a good low card, but it will too often get you into too much trouble. If you're playing sixty-four and have a borderline call with a low hand that contains a 5, fold fast. In a game with seven loose players, a sixty-five will either lose or tie more often than it will win. And remember that you get only a quarter of the pot if you tie an opponent for low, and you lose all if you tie on a swing.

The staying requirements for tight play include:
1. Two or three wild cards.
2. A wild card and two cards to a perfect low.
3. A wild card and a pair of natural aces, kings, or queens.
4. Three natural aces. But fold trip kings or queens if anyone bets vigorously; it's too easy for low hands to develop into four or five aces.

BEAT YOUR NEIGHBOR

Although this betting-in-the-blind game is a lot of fun in penny ante, it offers no opportunity for bluffery, carding strategy, or poker analysis. Each player receives five cards down, but does not look at any of them. The player to the left of the dealer turns up one card. A betting interval. Then the next player turns up one or more cards until he beats the first player's card. When he does top it, there is a second betting interval. Then the third player turns up until he beats the second player's up cards, and so on. (Note that when any player turns up five cards without beating the man to his right, he is automatically out of the pot.) Eventually, the turning gets back to the player who exposed the first card. If he has called all bets, he can turn additional cards until he beats the first active player to his right. Then the turning goes to the next active player with remaining down cards, and so on until all the cards are up.

Often the dealer and the players to his right will have to call a lot of bets before they see a single card to their own hand. It is best to fold in a latter position if a pair (especially a high pair) turns up early. Remember that it's about 50-50 that your hand will not contain any pair at all.

Also called No Peek, Beat Your Neighbor is often played at the end of poker sessions to settle odd chips. Played thus, it is a showdown game for a fixed amount, without betting intervals.

BEDSPRINGS

Each player receives five cards face down, as in draw forms. Then two rows of five cards each are dealt face down in the widow. These cards will be turned up one at the time, with a betting interval following each turn. When all widow cards are up, each active player may choose two cards that are contiguous crosswise. A diagram will probably be clearer:

```
    A . . . . . . 2
    4 . . . . . . 5
    6 . . . . . . K
    Q . . . . . . J
   10 . . . . . . 3
```

The horseshoe arrow indicates the direction in which the cards are turned up. In this example, the ace is turned up first. The 4, second. The 6, third. . . . The deuce, last. After the cards are up, each active player may use either A-2, 4-5, 6-K, Q-J, or 10-3 in his poker hand.

The final hands run somewhat higher than in Seven-Card Stud. But the playing requirements are, or should be, much higher because there are so many betting intervals—10, in fact. Only triplets or two high pairs are worth playing.

Bedsprings is often played high-low. As in most other forms of poker, you should almost always shoot for low, especially in cards speak. And you really need four low cards in your original hand to play this game. If you stay with only three low cards, you'll have to call a lot of bets before you can make a low hand. For example, you hold 2-3-5-X-X in your hand and the widow cards are the ones shown in the diagram above. The first two turn cards give you four to a wheel, but you'll have to call eight bets before you finally do make a fifth low card.

Bedsprings is also called Hollywood.

BEST FLUSH

Here's one from *Poker: The Nation's Most Fascinating Card Game*: "A game in which only flushes may compete for the pot: the best fourflush if there is no flush, the best three or two cards of the same suit if there is no longer flush."

BET OR DROP

See Pass and Out.

BETTY HUTTON

Seven-Card Stud with the 5's and 9's wild. The average winning hands run slightly less than in Baseball because in Betty Hutton there is no free down card on an exposed 4-spot (or its equivalent).

On the go, playable hands include two or three wild cards, natural triplets, one wild card with an ace or king, a pair of natural aces, and three cards to a straight flush. Unless the betting is nominal, fold the last three hands if the next card up doesn't help them.

BIG SQUEEZE
See Substitution Poker.

BLIND STUD
Sometimes called Mike and Racehorse, this is a form of poker in which all the cards are dealt down, but there is no draw. It can be played with five, six, or seven cards. The average winning hands are about the same as for Five-, Six-, or Seven-Card Stud.

In the seven-card form, each player receives three down cards before the first betting interval occurs. Down card, bet. Down card, bet. Down card, bet. Final down card, final bet. The staying requirements are the same as for Seven-Card Stud.

In the six-card form, each player receives two down cards before the first betting interval. Down card, bet. And so on until six cards are down. The staying requirements are the same as for Six-Card Stud. In this game, never call on low two-card straights and flushes.

In the five-card form, each player receives two down cards before the first betting interval, and the game proceeds as in the six-card form until each active player has five down cards. The staying requirements include any pair, two high cards, or an ace with a middling card.

Generally, Blind Stud builds good pots, but it is of course more of a gamble than the regular stud forms. Also, it doesn't give the expert as much opportunity for card analysis and strategy.

BLINDS AND STRADDLES
See Blind Tiger.

BLIND SPIT
This variation is dealt exactly like ordinary Spit-in-the-Ocean except that the wild card is not turned up until after the draw. It doesn't get as much action from conservative players because half the betting is done pretty much in the dark. A high natural pair,

triplets, or possibly a one-card draw to a straight flush are the only hands worth playing in conservative sessions.

BLIND TIGER

At one time, draw poker in which the man under the gun (called the age) had to open in the blind was the most popular game in this country. Today, it is not played nearly as often as Jacks or Straight Draw. In England, South Africa, and Australia, however, a form of blind opening in which a player who raises in the blind can double the preceding bet (called doubling or straddling) is the predominant form of draw.

Blinds and straddles loosen up the game somewhat, and sand-bagging is all but eliminated because no one can check before the draw (called the buy in England). But, generally, the winning hands and the staying requirements are the same as for Jacks.

One interesting situation shapes up when you have had to blind it and no one has called a straddle. You are left head to head with a player who has raised without seeing his cards. Remember that it's almost a 50–50 chance that he doesn't have even a single pair. So call if you hold deuces or even A-K. Raise on a pair of 8's or better. The same situation occurs when you deal and no one has straddled or called the blind.

There are of course some fine points in such games as Blind Tiger. For most American dealer's choice sessions, the discussion under Jacks, if properly adapted, along with the discussions of bluffing, carding, and so on in Part One, will be adequate to put you a notch or two above your opponents. But if you're going abroad for action, you may need a good deal more finesse. Read some of the British texts, such as Maurice Ellinger's *Poker: How to Play and Win;* Terence Reese and Anthony Watkins' *Poker: Game of Skill;* or Hubert Phillips' *Profitable Poker.*

BULL

A seven-card game with seven betting intervals. Each player receives three down cards. First bet. Up card; second bet. Up card; third bet. Up card; fourth bet. Up card; fifth bet. Then each active player rolls one of his down cards; sixth bet. Another roll; seventh bet. Showdown.

Bull is often played high-low. The winning hands are the same as for Seven-Card Stud High-Low—but the staying requirements should be a little more stringent because of the additional betting intervals.

BUTCHER BOY

Here's one from Albert H. Morehead's *The Complete Guide to Winning Poker:* "All the cards are dealt face up, one at a time. When a card of the same rank as a previously dealt card shows up, it is transferred to the player who was previously dealt that rank, giving him a pair. There is then a betting interval, and the deal is resumed with a face-up card to the player from whom the card was transferred (or, if he has dropped, to the next active player in turn). The deal continues in this way, with a betting interval after the transfer of each card, and the pot goes to the first player to get four-of-a-kind.

"How to play: Don't—unless you are closer to making four-of-a-kind than anyone else. Since this strategy will have a stultifying effect on the game, Butcher Boy is a poor choice unless the game is a casual one."

CALIFORNIA

See Cincinnati.

CALIFORNIA LOWBALL

A form or scale for low poker in which A-2-3-4-5 is the best possible low hand. See Low Poker.

CANADIAN STUD

See New York Stud.

CINCINNATI

A popular widow game. Each player is dealt five cards face down, as in draw forms. Then five more cards are dealt face down in the widow. These are turned up one at the time, and a betting interval follows each turn. In most circles, the first betting interval takes place before any of the widow cards are turned.

Full houses are common in Cincinnati, and four-of-a-kind are not too rare. But a flush will stand up quite often *if* a pair does not show in the widow (and it's about 50–50 that a pair will be turned up). It is not advisable to play for a flush, however, except as incidental to triplets or two high pairs.

More often than not, Cincinnati is played high-low. And it is a very good high-low game because the opportunities for swinging are frequent. Since you can use any five cards for high and any five for low, it's entirely possible to end up with a full house *and* a wheel.

The probabilities for making the various hands in Cincinnati and similar games are listed in Table VIII in Part Two, page 115. A cut and dried list of staying requirements would be cumbersome because there are so many possibilities. But, generally, you'll need at least three wheel cards to stay for low.

Even when you hold four low cards in your hand, slow down when a widow card pairs one of them. This card, in effect, lowers the value of your low hand considerably because it possibly helped all other low hands except yours. Thus, A-2-3-X-X with a king as the first widow card is a fairly good playing hand, but it is no good at all if a deuce is the first widow card. Remember also that you can lose money even on a perfect low hand in Cincinnati. Consider what happens in a five-handed game when four players have an ace down and 2-3-4-5-X turns up in the widow. They all play low, since they have wheels. A fifth player, however, holds queens full and goes high. He will get half the pot, and the low players split the other half four ways, thereby getting back 62½¢ on the dollar

A high pair and two low cards to a perfect low are worth a call if the betting is modest. Fold, however, if the first turn card doesn't make triplets or further your low hand.

Triplets and two low kickers are definitely worth playing. Three aces along with two low cards are worth a raise, since any low card in the widow will either make you a high full house or further your low hand.

Two pairs down should not be played, in very tight high-low sessions, unless they are also potential swing cards, such as A-A-3-3-6 or 5-5-2-2-3. In looser play, where the pot offers better odds, two high pairs, such as K-K-Q-Q-X are worth a modest call.

Never play on a fourflush that doesn't have low potential, preferably with an ace working in the flush. If you do fill the flush, do not jeopardize a good low hand by swinging in chips declare or consecutive declaration if a pair shows in the widow, or if the betting indicates strength around the board. Also, beware of swinging on a low flush if three cards of another suit show in the widow. Generally, a flush is indeed a valuable bonus in cards speak, but not in declaration forms of high-low.

Some players make a distinction between Cincinnati and a game called Tennessee. The only difference is that in Tennessee the widow cards are turned off the deck one by one instead of being dealt face down en bloc and then turned up one by one. Cincinnati is also called Utah, Lamebrains, and California.

CINCINNATI LIZ

This game is dealt exactly like Cincinnati except that the lowest card in the widow (and all like it) is wild. The trouble with Cincinnati Liz is that the wild card often changes several times while the widow is being turned. Thus, you can have five-of-a-kind on one turn and only a full house on the next.

Generally, your most stable hand shapes up when a very small card shows in the widow early and you have one like it in your hand. Or when you hold high triplets down. The possibilities of high triplets depend on how low your kickers are. If you hold A-A-A-K-Q, there is almost no chance that the king or queen will pair the lowest card in the widow; consequently, pairing the king or queen will not improve your hand, since the wild card in the widow will make you four aces. (Four aces will win some pots, but don't get excited about anything less than five-of-a-kind in Cincinnati Liz.) But if you hold A-A-A-2-3, pairing either the deuce or the trey in the widow will give you an unbeatable hand.

Cincinnati Liz is also called Lamebrain Pete. There is a similar game, called Telephone, that I like much better. In this version, the lowest card in your *hand*, not in the widow, is wild. Thus, if you hold A-A-A-K-Q and a queen shows in the widow, you have five aces no matter how many lower cards turn up. Clearly, Telephone is a more stable game. Natural triplets (high ones) or a pair of wild cards are the minimum staying requirements in tight play.

In another version, which is sometimes called Omaha, the dealer places a chip on any one down card in the widow. This card (and all like it) becomes wild when it is turned up.

CHICAGO

Chicago is dealt exactly like Seven-Card Stud. The big difference is that the high spade *in the hole* wins half the pot. The probabilities for making the various poker hands in Seven-Card Stud will apply to Chicago—but the minimum staying requirements are much more stringent because the high hand wins only half the pot. In my opinion, anything less than triplets or a pair of aces on the first three cards should be folded at once unless you also have a high spade in the hole. But perhaps I'm a little jumpy about this game. I still remember losing $40 in a $2-limit game on kings full with the ♠K down. Someone had the ♠A, and another player made four-of-a-kind without a pair showing!

The very best hand, of course, contains the ♠A down. But the probability of catching this pigeon on the first two down cards is only 0.038. When the ♠A shows around the board, then the ♠K becomes high spade. When both the ♠A and the ♠K show, then the ♠Q reigns. And so on. Many loose players string along on a ♠10 or even a ♠9 in the hole, in hopes that the higher spades will be exposed before the deal is concluded or that they will catch a higher spade down the river. This folly will cost them money over the long haul. Playing a mediocre spade is sound only if you also have a good shot for the high money, and playing a mediocre hand is sound only if you have a high spade. These mediocre hands will sometimes win all the pot—but if the pot is large, mediocre hands will usually lose both ways.

Whenever you are lucky enough to hold the lock spade in the hole at the outset, I recommend that you sandbag for a few rounds. It is by far better to have five players call a $2 bet than to have one player call a $10 bet—unless you have a good high hand as well as lock spade. Assuming that the pot will be split, you will win $5 if five players call a $2 bet, but you won't win a penny on the betting interval in question if only one opponent calls a $10 bet and wins high money.

If you have a good chance to win both ways, you may want to slow play until some money gets into the pot. Then bet heavily to drive out as many players as possible, thereby increasing your chances of winning all the money.

Sometimes Little Chicago is played, with the low spade taking half the pot. Usually, the deuce is low, but some circles let the ace count low for spades and high in pairs.

Chicago is a lot of fun in loose games. But it doesn't get much action in conservative sessions simply because tight players get the hell out if they don't hold a good high spade or an exceptionally good poker hand.

CRISS CROSS
See X-Marks-the-Spot.

DEUCES WILD
Ordinary draw poker. Deuces are wild. The main point to remember is that the more deuces you hold, the fewer your opponents can have. A deuce and two natural aces, then, make a stronger playing hand than three natural aces. Generally, it is unsound to play unless you do hold a deuce, except when you catch a pat hand or high natural triplets. The staying requirements and advice below are based on a fairly loose game.

Hands to Play
1. 2-2-X-X-X. Two wild cards going in are worth a raise regardless of what the other three cards are. The average winning hand in Deuces Wild is high triplets, and two wild cards automatically give you triplets of some sort. Generally, it is best not to hold a kicker smaller than an ace when you are drawing to two wild cards; but if the carding indicates that your opponent holds triplets, you may want to hold a king kicker. If the three cards with your deuces contain a pair, hold it. Do not be tempted to split a natural pair to draw one card to a straight flush. But if the other three cards to your two deuces make either a straight or a flush, hold pat. Raise before the draw. Straights and flushes are pretty good hands in Deuces Wild, and the fact that you hold two wild cards increases their value. If a player holds pat in front of you, however, throw a small or middling straight away and draw to your two deuces.

2. A-A-A-X-X. Raise on trip aces. Call on court triplets. Fold any natural triplets smaller than 10's unless the pot offers good odds and the betting has been modest.

3. 2-A-A-X-X. Raise on two natural aces and a deuce. Call on a deuce and a pair larger than 9's. If the betting is not strong, call on a deuce and a low pair—but fold them after the draw unless you improve.

4. Pat straight. Raise before the draw, and play for position. Ideally, you'll want to be the last to speak after the draw.

5. Pat flush. Raise before the draw. Bet after the draw if it's checked to you. Fold after the draw if the carding and betting indicate that the flush is beaten.

6. Four to a straight flush. Draw. If the straight flush is open on both ends, you have an almost even chance of making a straight or better, and your chances are considerably increased if you hold a deuce.

7. 2-2-2-X-X. Sandbag. Slow play. You hold all but one of the wild cards; therefore, vigorous betting will be likely to drive out most of the players. You automatically have four-of-a-kind, so let some of your opponents stay in.

8. J-J-J-4-4. Raise on any pat full house. Bet it after the draw.

Traps to Avoid

1. A-A-X-X-X. Fold any single pair, including aces. You have to make at least triplets to win—and sometimes making triplets would just get you in trouble.

2. A-A-3-3-X. Fold any two pairs. The hand doesn't figure to win as is, and the chances of improvement are too slim.

3. 2-3-6-9-J. Fold a single deuce with four trash cards. Really, you don't *have* to play just because you hold a wild card.

4. Fourflush. Fold.

5. Possible straights. Fold.

♥ ♥ ♥

Table I in Part Two, page 108, shows some interesting quirks in the mathematics of Deuces Wild. First, there are 30,816 sets of four-of-a-kind, but only 12,672 full houses. This means that a full house should rank above four-of-a-kind in Deuces Wild, but of course it doesn't. There are only 13,204 flushes, and these too should rank above four-of-a-kind. Also, two pairs (95,040) should rank above triplets (355,056).

About half the total number of pat hands are straights (66,236);

consequently, if you hold a full house against another pat hand, it is a better than even chance that your opponent will hold only a flush or a straight. But if your opponent indicates strength by betting into your pat hand after the draw, or by raising your bet—watch out. You have to put him on something stronger than a straight or a flush. It's about 3 to 1 that he holds four-of-a-kind or better *if* his hand is stronger than a flush!

DR. PEPPER

A draw game with 10's, 2's, and 4's wild. Straight flushes will win some pots, but don't make a habit of raising on anything less than five-of-a-kind after the draw. The only hand worth a re-raise is five aces.

It is difficult to give specific advice on the playing requirements for Dr. Pepper because anything can happen. Much depends on how loose the play is and on how large the ante is in relation to the bets. The following pointers will apply to a loose game with low limits and a reasonable ante.

1. Normally, you'll need at least two wild cards to play, but if the bet is small in relation to the size of the ante, a single wild card is sometimes worth a four-card draw.

2. Three natural aces or kings are worth a call, but are not as good as two wild cards, which have more possibilities.

3. If you hold two natural cards to a straight flush along with two wild cards, it is usually best to forget the straight flush and draw three.

4. If you draw to three wild cards, an ace is the only kicker worth holding, and even an ace should be discarded if the play indicates that you may be bucking a pat straight flush.

5. When you hold two wild cards and a small pair, throw in the pair and draw three.

6. Raise on a pat straight flush before the draw, but play it cautiously after the draw if two or more opponents stay in.

7. Raise on any set of fives going in, but proceed cautiously on anything less than five jacks after the draw. If you happen to hold five aces before the draw, you may choose to sandbag when your position is bad. (If you let everybody draw, however, you may end up splitting the pot with another opponent who also makes five aces!)

8. Raise on four aces—but not four kings—before the draw. They may hold up without improvement if you can drive out some of the players.

♥ ♥ ♥

Dr. Pepper is sometimes played in the form of Seven-Card Stud. In this variation you need at least one wild card on the go. A pair of natural aces is worth a call if it's cheap, but fold if the fourth card doesn't make you triplets. After the first betting interval, the staying requirements will vary considerably from deal to deal, depending on how many wild cards are out and how they are distributed around the board.

As in Dr. Pepper draw, straight flushes will win some pots. But, again, the only powerhouse is five aces.

DOUBLE–BARRELED SHOTGUN
See Texas Tech.

DOUBLE TROUBLE
See Hurricane.

DOWN THE RIVER
See Seven-Card Stud.

DRAW POKER
A standard form of poker in which all the cards are dealt face down. It is often called Closed Poker. The more popular draw games include Jacks, Lowball Draw, Deuces Wild, and Spit-in-the-Ocean.

See Chapter 6 for a discussion of carding strategy in Draw Poker, and Chapter 5 for positional strategy. For other poker forms, see Stud Poker and Widow Poker.

EIGHT–CARD STUD
This game usually starts off like Seven-Card Stud, but it ends up with an additional down card and betting interval. Although there are variations on the mechanics of the deal, (such as three cards down, four up, one down), each player who remains active all the way ends up with four down cards and four up cards.

The staying requirements are the same as for Seven-Card Stud. Straights and flushes will usually win if they connect. But full houses are not at all uncommon—especially when several open pairs show around the board.

ENGLISH STUD

Each player receives two hole cards and one up card. First betting interval. Second up card. Second betting interval. Third up card. Third betting interval. Each active player now has five cards— two down, three up. At this point, a substitution round begins. In turn, each active player can either hold pat or discard and draw either an up card or a down card. Fourth betting interval. Another substitution round. Fifth betting interval. Showdown. If a player stands pat on the first substitution round, he cannot draw the second time around.

The playing requirements are the same as for Seven-Card Stud— but the winning hands run slightly lower because each player ends up with only five cards, thereby eliminating some incidental straights and flushes from being filled while playing on pairs and triplets. Triplets will often win.

Discarding is sometimes tricky, as when you hold a high pair and four cards to a flush. If you shoot for the flush, you'll have to split the pair; if you hold the pair, you'll have to throw away a flush card. In this case, draw to the flush if the up cards and play indicate that it will take a flush to win. If the pair is exposed, it's usually better to hold it; if you split it, the other players will know that you are going for a flush, and after the substitution they will know whether or not you hit it. For example, you hold (♦-♦)/♣K-♦K-♦2. Discarding the ♣K will lay your hand wide open.

This game is highly developed in England, where, according to Terence Reese and Anthony T .Watkins in *Secrets of Modern Poker*, it is the only stud game allowed in most London gambling clubs. It is also quite popular in South Africa and Australia. So, if you're going to any of these countries, deal out a few hundred practice hands of English Stud before you take on the local talent.

FIVE AND TEN
See Woolworth.

FIVE–CARD STUD

Everyone who has watched TV and movies knows how to deal this one, so I'll skip the mechanics. What to play in Five-Card Stud depends largely on the betting limits and the number of players in the game. In high-stakes action, it is best to fold unless you have an ace, a king, a pair, or two cards higher than 9. Some experts play by the 19 rule; that is, they fold whenever their first two cards don't add up to at least 19 (counting face cards as 10 and aces as 11). An ace is a very good card in Five-Card Stud, and A-K or A-Q will sometimes win without improvement. But if you play an ace and a low card, it is by far better to have the ace in the hole.

The ideal situation in Five-Card Stud is to pair your hole card, so that the strength of your hand will be concealed. As Table VII in Part Two, page 114, shows, the probability of pairing your hole card varies significantly with the number of players in the game and the up cards they catch; consequently, it is important that you remember the cards that have been folded around the board. Remember *all* the cards, not just the ones that would have helped your hand, so that you can assess your opponents' chances of improvement. Card memory is more important in Five-Card Stud than in any other well-known poker game.

A small pair back to back, or on the first three cards, presents difficult problems. Against a single opponent, you probably have a winner with any pair unless he has a higher pair showing. Against seven opponents, you will more than likely have to help a low pair to win. And it's difficult to improve a pair back to back. My advice, for high stakes play, is to fold a small pair if you do not trip it on the second up card and do not catch an ace or a king for a scare card. If you don't have a scare card, the betting is likely to become prohibitively heavy for you to continue on your small pair. In limit play, however, you may want to continue regardless of what you catch.

Table VII shows the probability of improving a small pair. Here is another useful table, taken from John R. Crawford's *How to Be a Consistent Winner in the Most Popular Card Games.*

As Crawford emphasized, the figures are based on the assumption that all five cards have been dealt. The table indicates that a low pair, even deuces, figures to win in a head-to-head game. A pair of 7's

PROFIT OR LOSS IN A HUNDRED POTS OF STUD

Pair	Number of Players in Pot							
	2	3	4	5	6	7	8	9
Deuces	Even	−25	−50	−70	−82	−89½	−94	−96½
Sevens	+32	+30½	+14	−15	−25	−44	−56	−68½
Tens	+54	+77	+80	+72½	+59	+43½	+24	+8
Queens	+68	+113	+140	+152½	+155	+152	+140	+129½
Aces	+83	+150½	+206	+250	+284	+309½	+328	+341

figures to win against three opponents. A pair of 10's, against even eight opponents. But this does not mean that you should play 10's all the way come hell or high water. The value of a pair of 10's, or most any other pair, depends largely on how many higher cards show around the board; thus, a pair of 10's is a very good hand against four opponents if only nonpaired pip cards show, but it is not so good if your opponents show a jack, a queen, a king, and an ace. Your pair of 10's would be pretty good, however, if four opponents showed two jacks and two queens, which would greatly reduce their chances of making a pair higher than 10's because they have some of each other's cards.

A time-tested rule for Five-Card Stud is that you should fold whenever you are beaten in sight. (A fairly common exception is in low-limit poker where the bet is small in relation to the pot, and a less common exception occurs in table stakes play when you have already bet most of your stack.) The really expert player, who knows his opponents and all the tricks of hole card reading, will fold whenever he believes that he is beaten, whether in sight or not.

Another time-tested rule is that you should bet the pot, or else the maximum limit, when you have the best hand. In other words, make them pay to draw out on you.

It is seldom advisable to bet or raise into a possible lock. For example, you hold (A)/A-10-6-9. Your opponent bets on (?)/K-J-4-J. You do not have a raise, and probably don't even have a call in heads-up play for high stakes. In this case, you have to credit your opponent with *something* of value in the hole if he is a competent stud man; since he stayed all the way (pairing jacks only on the last card) he probably has either an ace, a king, a queen, or another jack in the hole. Maybe a 10. The purely mathematical odds would be quite high against his having a king or another jack, but what are the odds against his playing all the way without holding a good high card in the hole? If you kept count of all the court cards that were folded during the development of the hand, you could come up with a set of odds based on the assumption that he had to have a high card to play. But even this set of odds would be, or should be, overridden by a fact.

The fact is that he bet his jacks into you, and he must have been worried all the way about that ace among your up cards. If he does not have another jack or a king in the hole, he would have nothing to gain by betting into you because you could not call *unless you could beat the jacks*. So fold fast unless you have reason to believe that he is bluffing or making an unsound bet for the purposes of long-term strategy.

Before you call "to keep him honest," I want to make a side bet. If he is a tight stud man and if you have been betting your exposed ace, I'll lay two to one odds that he's got either an ace or a king down. If he didn't have either an ace or a king in the hole, he would be violating the first rule of Five-Card Stud: fold if you can't beat what you see around the board!

I indicated above that your opponent would not have bet if he couldn't beat your aces. But there are times when you should bet into a possible lock. For example, you hold (K)/9-J-K-3. Your opponent has (?)/10-6-8-9, a possible straight. If he knows his stud and the game is honest, bet into him. If he raises, call. Why? Because no competent stud player would have called the first bet with a 7 in the hole. Even if he started off with such a hole card, he would have folded on the third card (if the betting was at all significant) because if he called at that point he would have to hit two gut shots to make the straight. He probably has 10's wired and hopes that you have 9's, or else he started off with an ace in the hole and is now bluffing. If he does have the straight, don't worry about losing the hand to him. You'll get your money back before the session is over!

♥ ♥ ♥

In some groups, a player may turn up a deuce or a trey and get a new hole card. This livens up Five-Card Stud slightly by keeping a player or two in from time to time. If you have an ace or a king showing, then pay for a new hole card if it doesn't cost too much. But don't play just because you *can* get a new hole card.

In still other groups, you can get a new hole card on the end, no matter what you hold. If for some reason or other you've played all the way without making a pair, then get a new hole card unless you're running a hand. When it's fairly obvious to the other players that you have paired a small or middling hole card, then turn it up on the end and get a new one so that they will not know it when you connect with triplets or two pairs.

Attempting to liven up Five-Card Stud, many groups allow such nonstandard hands as blazes and flashes into the rank of poker combinations. These hands are covered under Special Hands. Also see New York Stud.

♥ ♥ ♥

A word of caution. Much of the professional cheating that I've seen has been at Five-Card Stud. A second dealer is murder in this game, simply because so much depends on so few cards. If he manages to deal himself or his accomplice a pair of aces or kings in Cincinnati Liz, he hasn't necessarily done too much to you; but it's hard to beat a dealer who can control the distribution of aces and kings in Five-Card Stud.

On the other hand, Five-Card Stud is really a classic game and many people prefer it to any other, especially for high stakes. My above statements about cheating are meant to be, as I said, a word of caution, not an intimidation.

FIVE–CARD STUD HIGH–LOW

The mechanics of the deal for this game are exactly like Five-Card Stud. The only difference is that the high hand and the low hand split the pot at the showdown.

In most high-low games, you are better off playing for low. But this one is an exception. Go for high. The reason is that the value of a low hand can change radically and irrevocably on any up card. A pair or a court card can completely bust a low hand, whereas a good high hand cannot be lowered. If you do shoot for low, it's best to have an ace, preferably in the hole. Against a single opponent, in cards speak, it's difficult (but not impossible) to lose both ways when you hold an ace. If you hold (A)/5-6-2-8 and your opponent holds (?)/7-4-8-3 in mixed suits, you can't lose in cards speak. If he has a 2, 5, or 6 in the hole, you win all the money. If he holds an ace down, you win low money with an eighty-six and he wins high money with A-8-7 against your A-8-6. So, an ace is a mightly good card to have in this game. Remember also that a pair of aces can swing, since it is both the lowest and the highest pair. Occasionally a straight or a flush will connect and swing, but the probability of making either of these hands in five cards is very low.

The staying requirements for conservative play are a high pair, an ace and a king, or an ace along with a low card. A pair of aces wired is the best hand on the go. Be sure to fold a low pair in table stakes or pot limit poker. (What will you do with a low pair when an opponent with an exposed ace taps or bets the pot? You won't know whether he's going high, low, or both ways.) In fixed limit games, you may want to gamble with a small pair in those family pots.

See Sudden Death for a discussion of playing low only in Five-Card Stud.

FLIP

See Mexican Stud.

FOLLOW THE QUEEN

A Seven-Card Stud game in which the card (and all like it) that falls immediately after a queen is wild. If two or more queens are dealt up, the card following the last queen is the wild one. Thus, it is not uncommon for the wild card to change once or twice in the course of a hand. Also, it is entirely possible that no queen will show, in which case there is no wild card.

Follow the Queen is rather unstable, so that high triplets make the only really good playing hand on the go. In loose play, most players will stay on any high pair until they see the first queen and subsequent wild card.

FOOTBALL

A game similar to Baseball. The 6's and 4's are wild. The 4 is the penalty card, similar to the trey in Baseball. A deuce up gets you a bonus hole card. The staying requirements and strategy are the same as for Baseball, which see.

FOURFLUSH STUD
See New York Stud.

444
Each player receives four down cards and four up cards. All 4's are wild. There are several variations in the mechanics of the deal in 444. Some players deal four cards down at the outset. Some alternate one down and one up. Some deal two down, four up, and two more down. And so on. The more conservative players, however, will prefer to see at least four cards to their hand before the first betting interval takes place.

In 444, full houses are common and four-of-a-kind are not unusual. The staying requirements for conservative play are a wild card or high natural triplets on the first four cards. Two high pairs, or even a single pair of aces, are worth a chip or two in loose play. But fold two small pairs (lower than jacks up) immediately; filling up may just get you in trouble.

GRUESOME TWOSOME
See Hurricane.

GUTS TO OPEN
See Straight Draw.

HEINZ
A Seven-Card Stud game with playing requirements similar to Baseball. The 5's and 7's are wild, and both are penalty cards when dealt up. As in Baseball, it is wise not to pay a high penalty unless you have at least one wild card in the hole. See Baseball for staying requirements and strategy.

HIGH–LOW DRAW
This high-low game, dealt like ordinary Jacks, is best played with chips declare. Oral declaration doesn't work because there are no up cards to designate the high man. Cards speak works all right, but robs the game of some subtlety and high-hand strategy. Any

of the low scales can be used, but California Lowball will get more action.

Tables I, II, III, and IV in Part Two, pages 108–111, apply to High-Low Draw, but the staying requirements for high are not the same as for Jacks and the staying requirements for low are not the same as for regular Lowball Draw. The reason for caution is that you don't know how many of the active players are going which way; in other words, you don't know what sort of competition you'll have, and there are no up cards to indicate which way a heavy raiser is likely to be playing. Staying hands include:

1. Four low cards. One of your best draws is a small bobtail, such as 2-3-4-5 or a low fourflush with the ace swinging, such as ♦ A-2-5-6. If you make the straight or the low flush, swing unless you have a very good reason to believe that you are beaten.

If you end up with an 8-high straight, or a flush with an 8 low, be careful about swinging against one or two raisers. Generally, you'll have a better chance for high with these hands unless you have reason to believe that the raisers are also shooting for high. Mathematically (but disregarding the cards that you actually hold), there are 56,458 hands that will beat an 8-7-6-5-4 for low, but only 15,636 that will beat the straight for high.

When you draw one card to a low hand and spike, consider the odds carefully before folding if the betting is modest after the draw. You may be able to back in for high, or even for low. Against a single opponent, you have almost a 50–50 chance of "guessing" right, and a better than 50–50 chance of winning if he draws one card or holds pat (because the majority on one-card draws and pat hands will be low ones). If you do spike, it's by far better to pair your highest card because you may win all the money if your opponent also pairs and also tries to back in for high! This sort of guessmanship is a lot of fun in low-limit play, but get the hell out if you don't make a sound hand in pot limit or table stakes. It's a matter of mathematics. When the pot contains $50 and your opponent bets it, you stand to lose $50 by calling but can win only $25 (half the pot if you guess right). You are therefore laying 2 to 1 odds that you can guess which way he's going. (See Chapter 7 for further discussions of this point.)

2. Triplets (or better). In cards speak, call on triplets, but don't

raise unless you fill up on the draw. In chips declare, raise before the draw to drive out as many players as possible. If you can narrow the opposition down to one or two players, hold pat and declare high. Your patsy will often be figured for low and your opponents may try to back in for high unless they made very good low hands. Of course this strategy will get you in trouble from time to time, but you will win more than you lose by trying it occasionally. Such a play will mix up your game, and will get you some calls when you do hit that good pat low hand. An alternate strategy for playing triplets is to draw one card (especially if the pat hand play is old hat in your group) and then raise after the draw. More often than not, your opponents will figure that you connected on a low hand.

One rule for chips declare: Always hold at least one kicker to triplets. If you draw two cards, your opponents will peg your high hand, especially if you're a conservative player who very seldom draws more than one card to a low hand.

3. Two pairs. The only two-pair hand worth playing in High-Low Draw is aces over.

In cards speak, call but don't raise unless you fill on the draw. If you end up against a single opponent who drew two or three cards, bet heavily after the draw. If he makes triplets, you win the low money. If he makes two pairs, you may win both ways with your swinging aces if your sidearms pair is lower than his highest pair; for example, you will win all the money in cards speak if you hold A-A-7-7-Q and your opponent holds J-J-5-5-K.

In chips declare, raise before the draw with aces over to drive out some of the opposition. Then hold pat and declare high, as when playing triplets. Again, the alternate strategy is to draw one card and raise after the draw.

4. Pat low hands. Raise on any pat seven, but go slow on a seventy-six if the carding and betting indicate real competition. What you do with a pat eight depends on how smooth it is, on your position, and (in cards speak) on whether or not you have an ace working. Fold a pat nine unless you are in ideal carding position and have an option to draw one card to a much better hand.

HIGH SPADE

This term designates a method of extrinsic betting on a poker deal. Two or more of the poker players put their wagers into a side pot, which is won by the participant who catches the highest spade. Unless it fills a flush, the high spade, as such, has no bearing on the poker hands.

Too much action on high spade distracts the players from poker and considerably slows down the game. Consequently, serious poker players usually discourage high spade and other such games of pure chance, which require no skill whatsoever. (Why give a sucker an even break?) Moreover, the bets at high spade often shoot up beyond all proportion to the limits of the poker game itself. But most players are sport enough to indulge in high spade on such occasions as determining who pays for the beer or who gets an odd chip from a split pot.

Sometimes low spade is played. The ace is high in most poker groups, but some do play it low. Ask.

HILO PICALO

See Take It or Leave It.

HOLD ME DARLING

This game, known also as Hold Me, was discussed at length in Chapter 8 to illustrate some of the principles of widow poker. Here's a brief recap of the mechanics: Each player receives two down cards. First betting interval. Three widow cards are turned up all together. Second betting interval. Fourth widow card is turned. Third betting interval. Fifth widow card. Fourth betting interval. Showdown.

Winning hands vary widely in Hold Me because so much depends on the widow. Each hand is different, and the first three turn cards set the scale. If, for example, three aces turn up right off in the widow, then the only really good hand would be four aces; if a pair of aces shows, trip aces would be good; if a single ace shows, a pair of aces would be good. When three hearts show, one or more players could easily have, or make, a flush. If all three cards are of mixed suits, flushes become improbable. When three cards in sequence show, one or more players could have, or make, a straight. Thus, the expert Hold Me player values his hand not by any fixed scale (as in Jacks) but on the scale set by the first three turn cards.

He also puts a lot of stock in overlays and kickers, as discussed in Chapter 8.

The staying requirements below apply only to seeing the first turn in an eight-handed game. An old pro once told me, "You have to make something on the turn. If you don't, get out." It is good advice.

1. Any pair is worth seeing the turn in low-limit play. The higher the pair, the better. With a very low pair, fold if you do not trip on the turn. With a high pair, fold if two or more overlays or an ace hit the board. In other words, play two jacks when something like 2-3-9 turn up but fold when something like A-K-8 turn up.

In high-stakes play, fold a small pair unless the betting is modest. Raise on a pair of queens, kings, or aces to discourage your opponents from playing potential straights and flushes—hands that could make two pairs on the turn. What you do with a high pair after the turn depends on how many active players remain and on what shows in the widow. When low cards show in the widow, bet. When an overlay shows—beware. When a smaller pair shows, think. For example, if you hold (Q-Q) and 3-3-J turn up in the widow, you have a bet coming *if your raise before the turn was substantial* because no one would have been likely to call with a trey in the hole; but when 3-3-A show, you may well be beaten if you have more than one opponent who called your raise before the turn.

When you hold aces down, you are much more likely to win without improvement because no widow card can overlay your pair. But you will not often win a really big pot with aces down, unless somebody calls a tap before the turn. The reason is that an ace will have to hit the board before you can hold a powerhouse, and widow aces tend to scare out the players who do not themselves have one down.

2. Any two cards to a flush are worth a call in low-limit play, unless there is a raise in front of you. In high-stakes play, call with two high flush cards, with an ace and a low card in suit, or with any two cards to a straight flush. Fold after the turn unless the widow continues your flush by at least two cards or makes at least one pair. Whether you continue playing on the strength of a pair depends on how much strength is shown and how many overlays show in the widow.

If you're lucky enough to fill the flush on the first turn, either raise or sandbag, depending on your position, the other active players, and so on. When you make a fourflush on the turn, you have an almost 50–50 chance of filling it on the next two turn cards. When you make a fourflush *and* a high pair, raise. When playing for any flush, however, take pause if a pair shows. A pair in the widow is a warning light flashing: FULL HOUSE, FULL HOUSE, FULL HOUSE.

3. Any two cards to a high straight are worth seeing the turn in limit play. An ace is a mighty good card to have in case you start pairing, but it decreases your chances of making a straight. With (10-J), for example, either 7-8-9, 8-9-Q, or Q-K-A combinations in the widow will fill your straight. But only 10-J-Q in the widow will fill your straight if you hold (A-K). In my opinion, which is the better hand on the go depends on the number of players in the game, as well as on the limits. In a loose low-limit game with eight or more players, I would prefer the (10-J) holding because of its higher probability of making a straight; in a tight high-limit game with fewer players, I would prefer the (A-K) holding because a pair of aces or kings, or even the A-K high, would be more likely to hold up.

In any event, fold after the turn unless you make at least one pair or continue your straight by at least two cards. Again, the value of a pair depends upon how high it is and how many overlays show in the widow.

When playing for straights beware of three cards of a suit, or a pair, showing in the widow. Just as a pair is a warning light for a full house, three cards of a suit is a warning light for a flush.

♥ ♥ ♥

Several widow games similar to Hold Me give each active player two down cards and five communal cards at the showdown. In a version called Omaha (or Tulsa) the widow cards are turned up one at the time, thereby adding two more betting intervals. The playing requirements are pretty much the same as for Hold Me, except that it's much more expensive to shoot for straights and flushes. Consequently, pairs and good high cards gain in significance. Fold two low straight cards on the go in tight play. Fold two flush cards unless they contain an ace or else are both higher than 10. Straight flushes, even low ones, are worth seeing a card or two if the betting doesn't get out of hand.

Another game, Amarillo, is dealt exactly like Omaha. The big difference is that you must play *both* hole cards in your poker hand. Thus, if you held (A-K) and Q-Q-Q-A-K was turned up in the widow, you would not have a full house.

The requirement of having to play both hole cards greatly reduces the average value of hands, and eliminates many straights and flushes. High cards in the hole have much more significance in Amarillo than in Hold Me or Omaha. As the example above shows, Amarillo is a tricky game. Even expert Hold Me strategists are advised to deal out a hundred or so practice hands of Amarillo before playing the game for high stakes.

HOLLYWOOD
See Bedsprings.

HURRICANE
This fast game is usually played high-low. Each player ends up with only two cards, so that a pair of aces is the best possible high hand and an A-2 is the best possible low hand. Sometimes deuces are played wild, in which case A-2 swings. Clearly, an ace (or a deuce in the wild card variation) gives one a decided advantage.

There are two ways of dealing Hurricane. In one form, each player receives only one down card before the first betting interval. Then the active players receive their second (and last) down card. There is another betting interval and a showdown. The staying requirements are simple: call on a low card. Raise on an ace (or a deuce in the wild version). Fold anything else. The chances of pairing a king or other high card are too slim. If you start off with an ace in cards speak, see the last bet no matter what you catch, unless the betting gets out of hand; an ace and a high card will often win high. If you go in with a deuce in the wild card version, play all the way no matter what you catch, unless, again, the betting gets out of hand. A cardinal rule for the deuces-wild version is never call the first bet unless you have either an ace or a deuce.

In the second form, each player receives two down cards before the first betting interval takes place. Then each active player has an opportunity to substitute one card before the second betting interval takes place. The conservative player will seldom draw unless he holds an ace (or a deuce). A pat three- or four-low is worth a play, and so is a high pair. But go cautiously on a pair of court cards in deuces wild, for an A-2 can swing on you.

Both of the above forms of Hurricane are sometimes called Gruesome Twosome.

Another variation, called Double Trouble, has three betting intervals. The first comes after each player receives his first down card. The second, after each active player receives his second down card. The third, after each active player has had an opportunity to discard and draw. The aces and deuces still have the advantage, and playing anything else becomes more dangerous—or more expensive—because of the added betting interval.

Still another variation is called Acey-Deucey. Here's a description from *Official Rules of Card Games:* "A form of two-card poker popular in the U.S. Army. Each player is dealt two cards, one up and one down. He may stand on the cards he is dealt, or at any later time, or he may draw by discarding one of his cards and being dealt a replacement (when his turn comes). If he discards a face-down card, the replacement is dealt face-down; if he discards a face-up card, the replacement is dealt face-up. If he draws one card he pays the pot one chip; for a second card, he pays two chips, and for a third card five chips. Betting begins when all hands have stood. High card bets, as in Stud Poker. The game is usually played high-low. Only pairs and high cards count [i.e., no straights and flushes count for high money]. Highest hand is A-A; lowest hand is A-2, since the ace is treated as low when the player tries for low (but A-A is never a low pair). Winners split the total pot, including the bets and chips paid to draw cards."

Also see Murder, a two-card game with *five* betting intervals!

INDIAN POKER
See Mexican Sweat.

JACKS
Most writers refer to this game as Jackpots. Most poker players know it as Jacks or Better to Open, and usually shorten it to Jacks

or Better—or simply Jacks. Anyhow, it's a standard draw game in which you must have at least a pair of jacks to open the pot.

But it's not always advisable to open on a pair of jacks. Or even queens, in some positions. It all depends on how many players are left to speak behind the opener. Here are the time-tested opening requirements (for sound play), which are also valid from a purely mathematical standpoint:

Players Yet to Speak	*Minimum Opening Requirements*
6	Aces (or K-K with A)
5	Kings (or Q-Q with A-K)
4	Queens
3 or less	Jacks

The *staying* requirements are a couple of notches above the minimum opening requirements; that is, if another player opens on jacks or better, you should normally have at least kings to call. Fourflushes and bobtail straights should be folded unless four or five players have called in front of you, which seldom happens in tight sessions. Possible straight flushes are worth a call against two or more opponents, but not against a single opponent.

Play short pairs only when sweeten antes have made the pot quite large in relation to the bet. Before making those loose calls on short pairs, remember that you have to improve to win—and remember also that your opponent has the same opportunity to improve that you have, so that improving short pairs may just get you in trouble, especially when you end up with *two* short pairs.

Over the long haul, how you play two low pairs before the draw probably determines whether you win or lose in Jacks and similar games. (By low pairs I mean anything lower than jacks over.) Any two pairs, no matter how low, figure to win against one or two opponents. Theoretically, you should bet or raise on low pairs before the draw to drive out as many players as possible. But two low pairs are not worth a bet *after* the draw (unless you fill up, and the odds are about 11 to 1 against it), so you must consider your betting position and what it will be after the draw. Obviously, you'll want to avoid being the one to open the pot. When you're under the gun or second to speak in a six- or seven-handed game, check. Then, if someone opens behind you, raise if you have no more than two active opponents. Of course your best position to drive out players shapes up when the man to your immediate right opens.

But you shouldn't always raise on two low pairs. Never raise when there is more than one caller between you and the opener; your two low pairs do not figure to win against three opponents, and your raise is not likely to drive them out, in limit play, after they have already called the opening bet. What do you do with your two low pairs in this case? Fold. Theoretically, you should always either raise or fold on two low pairs before the draw.

Carding on two pairs offers few stratagems. Most of the time you should draw one card, in an attempt to improve your hand. Hold pat if you want to discourage anyone from betting into you after the draw. In certain rare cases, it is correct to throw away one of the pairs and draw three cards! This unusual play was discussed in Chapter 6, along with the pros and cons of holding a kicker to a single pair or triplets.

Playing two high cards and small triplets presents some problems, but with these hands a bad position is not as precarious as when you hold two small pairs. Aces up, kings up, and small triplets figure to win without improvement against three active opponents. Consequently, your bets and raises on these hands should be geared to build the pot rather than to drive players out. But you don't want so many players that the fourflushes and bobtails will start drawing at you. So raise from any position before the draw, unless there has already been a raise in front of you. In tight play, consider folding small triplets if there are two raises (from competent players) in front of you, or if two conservative players call a substantial raise.

With high triplets, you may want to sandbag in the early positions. Your raises should definitely be geared to build the pot rather than to drive players out; consequently, slow play if the man to your immediate right opens. The ideal position before the draw is to have several callers between you and the opener, in which case you raise. The worst position after the draw shapes up when you have opened, or called immediately to the opener's left, and have two or three one-card draws behind you. If you bet into these one-card draws, you are liable to be clobbered by a flush. If you don't bet into them, you will lose money by letting those two-pair and low triplet hands have a free ride. This bad position is sometimes unavoidable, but remember that it can become the *best* position from which to build those really big pots in high-stakes play. If you have trip kings or aces, draw two and check to those one-card draws. When one or more of them connect with either a flush or a straight, or a smaller full house, they will bet out and then you find yourself in an ideal position to tap if you fill up or make four-of-a-kind! If you don't fill up, you'll have to determine whether your opponent (the one who bet into you) was shooting for a flush or held a triplet-kicker hand. Or maybe he is known to bluff frequently on busted flushes. If you think he really hit a flush or a straight, fold. If you think he was playing triplets with a kicker, raise. And sometimes you *can* tell pretty much what he was doing. Consider the following example:

The man on your immediate left is a steady, conservative player. On his deal, you catch three aces. No one opens in front of you. You almost have to open (no matter how bad your position will be after the draw) because the hand may well pass out if you sandbag. The dealer calls. The other players fold. You draw one and check. The dealer draws one and bets. You raise. Because he probably holds either triplets and a kicker or two high pairs. Since he is a conservative player, he wouldn't have drawn to a flush because the pot didn't offer anything like the right odds. In either case, he may call your bet. It could be argued that you should have bet into him in the first place. But the point is that you do have a bet or even a raise into such a one-card draw if you know your man, but not against a one-card draw to a fourflush or bobtail. The big difference is that you don't have anything to gain by betting into a possible flush or straight (unless you fill up) because your opponent will not call your bet unless he connects. If he does connect, he will raise.

Another problem—and one that you will want to face often!—is whether to draw or hold pat if you happen to catch four-of-a-kind. Drawing will help conceal the strength of your hand, because a one-card draw would indicate that you hold two pairs, triplets with a kicker, a fourflush, or a bobtail. In high-stakes poker, however, it is sometimes advisable to hold pat, thus representing a straight or a flush. If someone fills up or makes an ace-high flush, you can take him to the cleaners. I made this play back in 1952 and was lucky enough to run into kings full. Since then I have caught three sets of fours on the go in draw poker—but twice the dealer had called lowball!

Still another problem in Jacks is whether or not to split openers.

For example, you hold a pair of queens, one of which also makes you a fourflush. You open. The player on your left raises, and the rest of the players quit. Should you draw to the flush or to the pair of queens? In this case, neither. You are probably beaten and don't have a good gamble on the flush. Show your openers and fold without calling the raise. But if three or more players come in after the raise, the odds may be right for you to shoot for the flush. In this case you should split the openers—but, in general, don't split aces or kings unless you have good reason to believe that they are beaten going in. Remember that in Jacks and similar games the highest hand going in figures to be the highest hand at the showdown.

♥ ♥ ♥

Draw games similar to Jacks include Acepots, Pass and Out, Guts to Open, and Blind Tiger. Also see Progressive Jacks, Trips to Win, and Jacks Back. Tables I and III in Part Two, pages 108 and 110, give the probabilities for making the various hands and draws.

JACKS AND REVERSE
See Jacks Back.

JACKS BACK
Sometimes called Jacks and Reverse, or Jackson, this game proceeds exactly like ordinary Jacks. If no one opens for high on the first round, the game reverts to Lowball Draw. If no one opens for low, a new deal must be made, usually after sweetening the ante.

The playing requirements for high are the same as in Jacks; for low, the same as in Lowball Draw. The only exceptions are small straights and flushes. Obviously, a wheel is a much better low hand than high hand, and should therefore be checked during the first round. It's worth a raise for high, though, if someone else opens with jacks or better.

Usually, I'll sandbag an 8-6-X-X-X flush the first round because it's a fairly good low hand if no one opens for high. But an 8-7-6-5-4 straight is better played for high (in both the California and sixty-four scales) because it will beat only a slick nine or worse for low; there are 56,458 low hands that will beat 8-7-6-5-4 in the California scale as compared to 15,636 hands that will beat the straight for high.

In any event, act promptly when you hold a small straight or flush in this game; if you have to stop to figure out whether an eighty-seven flush works better for high or low, the opposition will quickly peg you for a pat hand.

Jacks Back is one of the better "Dealer's Choice" games, and is just the ticket to liven up a slow session of Jacks.

JACKSON
See Jacks Back.

JOKER POKER
Most wild card games have specific names, such as Baseball, Dr. Pepper, and Deuces Wild, but the joker is often added to the standard deck and is used in any of the "Dealer's Choice" games. Most groups play the joker as the "bug"; that is, wild as an ace or in filling straights and flushes. The bug is a very good card to hold in a game like Seven-Card Stud, where straights and flushes are not uncommon but are still fairly strong hands.

In some groups, the joker is completely wild, a condition that tends to kill the play in stud games, where an exposed joker gives the lucky recipient too much advantage and leaves the other players with no chance of also catching a wild card.

Other groups play the joker as the bug in high poker, but as completely wild in low poker. It is also a very good card to hold in low poker, when it's wild, because it not only furthers a low hand but also reduces the danger of spiking out.

Either the wild joker or the bug has a bearing on staying requirements for almost all games. Table I in Part Two, page 108, shows the possible hands with the joker and bug working. The bug has less effect than the joker, but it still increases the importance of aces because there are now five of them, as well as adding over 13,000 straights and flushes to the total number of poker hands.

I like to catch the bug often in a poker game, but I believe that it costs the average player more than it makes him over the long run. All of us tend to play too often and too far into a hand when we hold the bug. It's a mighty good card to have, but it doesn't make two small pairs a winning hand in Jacks and it doesn't improve three kings in Seven-Card Stud High-Low.

KANKAKEE

This one is Seven-Card Stud with a communal joker; that is, the joker is turned up in the center, is wild, and works in every active player's poker hand. When playing Kankakee, forget about straights and flushes. A high full house (two pairs in your hand plus the wild widow) will take some pots, but four-of-a-kind are as common as triplets are in Seven-Card Stud.

KNOCK POKER

This combination of poker and rummy is not a very good dealer's choice game. (For one reason, the dealer is at a disadvantage!) But it's ideal for two, three, or four players while waiting for the poker session to get started.

Each player receives five cards down, as in Jacks. The rest of the deck is then placed in the center, and the top card is turned up to start a "discard" pile. The player to the left (if he doesn't choose to knock at the outset) may either draw the top card off the deck or he may take the exposed card. Whichever one he chooses to take, he must then discard one face up onto the discard pile. Then the player to his left has the same option: top of the deck or top of the discard pile. Whenever a player feels that he has the best poker hand, he can knock. If he does have the best hand, he wins a chip (or whatever the stakes are) from each player; but if he doesn't have the best hand, he loses two chips to whoever beats him. There is obviously inducement for sandbagging, but, in, general, it's best to knock when you make a pat hand or whenever you are pretty sure that you hold a winner.

There are several variations of Knock, and all of them offer much room for strategy, analysis, and carding skill. I won't go into the fine points here, however, because, as I said, it really isn't a dealer's choice game. If you do play a lot of Knock, be sure to read the long discussion in *Esquire's Book of Gambling*. It's by far the best thing I've seen on this particular game.

LAMEBRAIN PETE

See Cincinnati Liz.

LAMEBRAINS

See Cincinnati.

LITTLE CHICAGO

A game in which the smallest spade in the hole wins half the pot. The mechanics of the deal are exactly like Seven-Card Stud. See Chicago for a discussion of playing strategy.

LITTLE SQUEEZE

Called Shuck 'em and who knows what else, this is one of the more common high-low substitution games. In his book *Poker for Fun and Profit*, Irwin Steig called it Little Squeeze. It's a fitting name. Whatever it is called, the game proceeds like Five-Card Stud High-Low. After the last up card has been dealt, however, each active player has an opportunity to discard either his hole card or one of his up cards and receive a replacement.

The trouble with Little Squeeze is that it gives the dealer too much positional advantage. He has so much the best of the game that it is foolish, in many cases, to contest him for low money. Consider an example in which all the other active players are going for high, except you and the dealer. Toward the end, you hold (A)/5-3-4-J. He holds (2)/6-7-10-2. You discard the jack, and the replacement card pairs your 5. (You almost had to draw, since you had no way of knowing that his exposed 2 paired his hole card.) The dealer now has a lock for low with his smaller pair. If he had been the first to substitute, he would have discarded one of the deuces and could well have caught a king or a queen or a card that spiked him. Then you could sit tight on your jack low. If he had caught the 5, you could come off your jack low and draw to beat his ten. Clearly, the first man to have to substitute is at a big disadvantage.

The playing requirements, in my opinion, vary according to your position in relation to the dealer. If you are under the gun or in an early position, play for high if you play at all. Steig recommends that you use the same playing requirements as for regular Five-Card Stud, but I want to point out that more straights and flushes will be filled in Little Squeeze than in Five-Card Stud High-Low (which is one of the few games in which you should always play for high instead of low). I feel, therefore, that low hands with swing potential are worth a play from a middle or latter position if the California low scale is being used. If you are the dealer, play any sort of hand that is in the running for low money.

For further discussion of tactics, position, and carding, see Substitution Poker and Five-Card Stud High-Low.

LOWBALL AND LOW POKER

Stand poker's hierarchic scale on its head and you have low poker, where the sorriest hand wins. Or that's the way it was when low poker was first played. Today, a new scale, based entirely on low cards without any carry-over from high poker, is about to become standard. This scale doesn't account for straights and flushes. The wheel (A-2-3-4-5) is the best possible hand. Low poker played by this scale is called California Lowball. (See the tabulation of California Lowball hands under Lowball Draw. Also see Tables II and IV in Part Two, pages 109 and 111.)

Two other scales are still used. In one, straights and flushes count against you, so that 6-4-3-2-A in mixed suits is the best possible low hand. This hand is sometimes called a royal six, but sixty-four (sixty-five, etc.) is the more common nomenclature. A sixty-four in one suit becomes a flush, so that you can completely bust your low hand when you draw one to four cards in suit.

The other scale is the seventy-five. Here aces are high only. Straights and flushes are high. The best possible low hand is 7-5-4-3-2 in mixed suits.

Of the three scales, I prefer California Lowball, usually, because it gets more action at the table. Playing straights and flushes high subtracts quite a few low hands from the total number of good low hands, and the danger of filling a straight or flush discourages players from drawing to some of the potential lows. Thus, in sixty-four, an A-2-5-6 is a strong playing hand, but 2-3-4-5 is not because either an ace or a 6 would bust the holding for low.

The California scale gives the expert an advantage in most high-low games because a straight or a flush can swing both ways, and the people who win the money at high-low year in and year out are the ones who play only potential swing hands. (But there are exceptions when good players play for high only.)

Almost any dealer's choice game can be played low, but the principal form is Lowball Draw. The principal form of high-low is Seven-Card Stud High-Low. These games are discussed in their alphabetical places, as well as in some of the chapters in Part One.

Generally, low poker is more of a gamble than high poker. You must bet more often on the come. But this is not quite like betting on the come in high poker because everybody else must also bet more often on the come in low poker, lest they ante all their money away. Lowball draw is less gamble than low stud forms simply because you see more cards to a complete poker hand before you bet. Sudden Death is probably the biggest gamble in all poker; a single card can ruin your low hand at any point, and you have no opportunity to draw for a better card.

LOWBALL DRAW

A standard draw game in which the lowest hand wins. The low scales vary somewhat from group to group, as explained in the discussion of Lowball and Low Poker above. By whatever scale, the cardinal rule for playing winning Lowball Draw is *do not stay in if you have to draw more than one card.* The only exception is when the pot is large in relation to the bet, as will happen occasionally when the antes accumulate because the pot has not been opened for several deals.

The author of a recent book, however, came up with some startling conclusions on Lowball Draw. His book is almost completely mathematical, and it seems very authoritative because he had access to an electronic computer for at least part of his calculations. His conclusions: Draw two cards to a potential 9 against two active opponents, and draw two cards to a potential 8 with more than two active opponents! This means that you would call against two active players each time you hold 9-8-7-K-Q. I can think of no faster way to lose your money in a heads-up session of Lowball Draw; yet the book is called *How Not to Lose at Poker*, by Mr. Jeffery Lloyd Castle. Personally, I don't care how Mr. Castle plays poker, but it's another matter when he publishes such advice. A reading of his text reveals that his figures are based on an ante that is *half* the bet; in other words, in a $20-limit game you would have to ante $10 each hand. That's much too high an ante for anybody to play good poker on a sound money management basis. Even with such a high ante, I still doubt that you should ever draw two cards to a ninety-eight when the stakes are substantial. Any pair or any high card could bust the hand. Even if you make your best possible hand, such a rough 9 will merely get you in trouble almost as often as not.

In my opinion, what you play and how you play it depends in large measure on your position at the table. Opening and staying requirements depend so much on position that, indeed, a particular hand is worth a raise in one position but should be folded in another. Positional strategy was discussed at length in Chapter 5 and will not be repeated here. (Also see the discussion of the percentage bet in Chapter 3.) In a normal game with a reasonable ante, about 95 percent of your bets and calls should be on pat hands and one-card draws to potential 8's or better. The probabilities of catching pat hands and making the various draws are listed in Tables II and IV in Part Two, pages 109 and 111.

♥ ♥ ♥

One mistake that many players make in low poker is in evaluating an 8 as one notch above a 7, and a 7 as one notch above a 6. Few people realize the significance of the second "countdown" card in each rank of lowball hands. Consider the chart on page 165 (for the California scale).

Remember that this chart represents only the *rank* of hands. The total *number* would be much, much higher; in fact, there are 1,024 possible hands in each rank. So, when the raises start you should count down closely before calling on a rough 8, much less a rough 9.

LOW HOLE CARD WILD

This game is dealt like Seven-Card Stud. The big difference is that the lowest card in the hole, and all like it in your hand, are wild. Thus, if you end up with (6-A)/A-6-5-K/(Q), you have four aces. But if your last down card (the queen) had been a trey, you would have ended up with only three aces. Clearly, the last down card can undercut your wild card unless your low hole card is a deuce. On the other hand, the last down card can sometimes improve your holding, but it's usually too much of a gamble to play that long without already having paired your low hole card, except when you hold something like (K-K)/K-10-5-6/(?).

The winning hands vary widely in Low Hole. A full house will take some pots, but only a straight flush or five-of-a-kind makes a really good hand. How vigorously you play your hand depends on what the other players have showing, but it is usually best to get out after the second up card unless you pair your low hole card, catch natural

8-4-3-2-A	7-4-3-2-A	6-4-3-2-A	5-4-3-2-A
8-5-3-2-A	7-5-3-2-A	6-5-3-2-A	
8-5-4-2-A	7-5-4-2-A	6-5-4-2-A	
8-5-4-3-A	7-5-4-3-A	6-5-4-3-A	
8-5-4-3-2	7-5-4-3-2	6-5-4-3-2	
8-6-3-2-A	7-6-3-2-A		
8-6-4-2-A	7-6-4-2-A		
8-6-4-3-A	7-6-4-3-A		
8-6-4-3-2	7-6-4-3-2		
8-6-5-2-A	7-6-5-2-A		
8-6-5-3-A	7-6-5-3-A		
8-6-5-3-2	7-6-5-3-2		
8-6-5-4-A	7-6-5-4-A		
8-6-5-4-2	7-6-5-4-2		
8-6-5-4-3	7-6-5-4-3		
8-7-3-2-A			
8-7-4-2-A			
8-7-4-3-A			
8-7-4-3-2			
8-7-5-2-A			
8-7-5-3-A			
8-7-5-3-2			
8-7-5-4-A			
8-7-5-4-2			
8-7-5-4-3			
8-7-6-2-A			
8-7-6-3-A			
8-7-6-3-2			
8-7-6-4-A			
8-7-6-4-2			
8-7-6-4-3			
8-7-6-5-A			
8-7-6-5-2			
8-7-6-5-3			
8-7-6-5-4			

Totals:	35	15	5	1

triplets, or have a one-card draw to a straight flush. Anything can happen on the last down card, but up until that event you can tell whether or not you have a lock at the moment; in other words, you can figure out the best possible hand that your opponent could hold.

In some circles, the dealer can, by announcement, serve the last card either up or "down and dirty" at each player's option. This takes some of the hazard out of this busting game and therefore gets more action from conservative players. I used to play with one group that allowed the dealer to serve your last card up if you first paid 50¢ to the pot.

McINTOSH

A Five-Card Stud game in which your hole card and all like it are wild *if* you pair it. Thus, (6)/A-6 would be three aces, but (6)/A-A would be only two aces because the hole card is not paired.

The game is complicated by a severe penalty ruling. If you make a pair up, you have to match the pot or fold. It is seldom advisable to match the pot, if it's of any size, unless you have also paired your hole card. In other words, seldom match the pot unless the exposed pair makes you four-of-a-kind.

MEXICAN STUD

This game is played exactly like Five-Card Stud except that all the cards are dealt face down. Each player selects his hole card and rolls the other one before each betting interval. Thus, one's hole card can be changed several times during the course of playing a hand. The winning hands and staying requirements are about the same as in Five-Card Stud—but Mexican Stud gives more room for strategy and bluffery. It's best to keep pairs and aces hidden as long as you believe that you hold the best hand. When you suspect that you are beaten, however, you may want to make a defensive play by exposing your pair or rolling up your ace.

Mexican Stud is also called Peep and Turn, Flip, and Pedro. See Shifting Sands for a discussion of Mexican Stud played high-low.

MEXICAN SWEAT

Sometimes called Indian Poker, this one is dealt like ordinary Five-Card Stud. The only difference is that you can't look at your hole card! The very idea of playing a blind hole card will bring a moan from every stud man in the country. But . . . well . . . your hole card isn't exactly blind. You see . . . uh . . . you can't look at *your* hole card but you can see everybody else's. The mechanics are a little awkward to explain, but it's really quite simple. You pick up your hole card very carefully with your right hand, lift it with its face out toward the center of the table, and place it on your forehead. You hold it there until the showdown.

In regular Five-Card Stud, the object is to pair your hole card. In Mexican Sweat, the object is to pair one of your up cards. If you do pair an up card, or have an ace up, you can tell for sure whether you hold a lock. Let's play a hand for fun. You hold (?)/A-2-2. Your opponent across the board holds (5)/J-Q-K. You don't know whether your hole card helps your exposed deuces, but your opponent does know. He doesn't know, however, whether he can beat even deuces, since he can't see his own hole card. You've got him guessing, even though you don't know the full value of your own hand. So, Mexican Sweat isn't a bad game, and it's a lot of fun to play in penny ante sessions.

MIKE

See Blind Stud.

MISSISSIPPI

Seven cards are dealt down, as in Anaconda (which is also another name for Mississippi). Each player discards two and then arranges the remaining five for roll 'em back. There are four rolls—with a betting interval following each one—so that the final hands look like Five-Card Stud. Mississippi is usually played high-low.

A seventy-five will usually take low money, but don't get too rambunctious on anything less than a sixty-four. For high, play full houses but not triplets. High straights and flushes will win some pots, but proceed very carefully if anyone shows a pair on the third roll. (Usually, but not always, a pair on the second roll indicates bluffery.)

As in most other high-low games, your best playing hand is a low flush or a very low straight, especially in cards speak with the California scale.

MURDER

Here's an interesting game from Irv Roddy's *Friday Night Poker*: "This is a fast little number that has only five rounds of bets but builds large pots. Considering the speed with which it is played, it becomes a stiff game. It is a two-card game with three substitutions. You pay for the substitutions the same as in three-card sub [Five-Card Stud High-Low with three substitutions on the end]. You are dealt a down card and bet and then an up card and bet. This is followed by the three substitutions with a bet after each trade. Ace is a high card only and straights and flushes don't count. Consequently, a pair of aces is a perfect high, and 3-2 is a perfect low, but the game has a gimmick. A pair of 7's takes the whole pot.

"An inexperienced player usually goes for the pair of 7's, but this is frequently the wrong play. If the first card dealt down to you is a 7, your chance of making a pair of 7's is roughly 1 in 5 for four tries, so it is incorrect to play for this pair unless you have five or more players staying for the first bet.

"In short, in a tight game, it is a bad gamble to play the 7 when you get one immediately. We will come back to the 7 shortly. You stay for the first bet on a 2, 3, 4, or an ace, with a 5, 7, or a king as an optional start when you have enough players in it. An ace is a powerful card in this game as it can win the high with any decent added card as A-J or A-9. A deuce or trey as your first card gives you a play for low or high. It can be paired on later rounds. A difficult problem is an A-2 on the first two cards; you must decide whether to go for high or low.

"It is sometimes correct to play the 7 in a loose game on the first card, but the beginner frequently makes this mistake. Pulling an ace for the second card, he continues to try for the whole pot; similarly with a low card, he plays for the 7's on later rounds. He does this even when another 7 is exposed, which greatly reduces the chance of pulling the pair. Once you get an A, 2, or 3 with a 7, it is a bad play to go for the whole pot."

NEW YORK STUD

Also called Canadian Stud or Fourflush Stud, this game is played exactly like Five-Card Stud except that a nonstandard hand is recognized: A fourflush will beat a pair, but not two pairs or better. The idea was, no doubt, to liven up Stud a bit. But holding back-to-back suit cards on the go is often a trap—an enticement to keep the suckers in. The probability of making a fourflush in the next three cards is only 0.109.

It is recommended, then, that suit cards be played only as incidental to one's standard playing requirements for Five-Card Stud. Most Stud players will see another card or two on, say, A-J; if these happen to be of the same suit, so much the better. In tight games for high stakes, play big cards in suit; fold the garbage, regardless of whether it is all red or all black. In a loose, low-limit game, when the pot offers better odds, two small suit cards may be worth a chip or two; if the third card is in suit, the probability of ending up with a fourflush is greatly increased.

In addition to the fourflush, some groups recognize a bobtail straight as a nonstandard hand. Usually, the bobtail will beat a pair but not a fourflush or better. In this variation of New York Stud, two low cards in suit and in sequence, such as ♠ 6-7, are worth a sporty play in loose sessions. There is a good deal of difference, however, between a 6-7 and a 6-8. With a 6-7, a bobtail can be made with a 4-5, a 5-8, or an 8-9. With a 6-8, only a 7-9 or a 5-7 will do the trick in two-card combinations (but there will be a remote chance of catching a 3-4-5 or a 9-10-J).

NO PEEK
See Beat Your Neighbor.

OMAHA
See Hold Me and Cincinnati Liz.

ONE–EYES WILD
On most modern brands of playing card, the ♥J and the ♠J are shown in profile, and, hence, have only one eye. These two jacks are popular as wild cards in some circles. The only other one-eye, the ♦K, is also used as a wild card, but not as often as the jacks.

In draw poker with one-eyed jacks wild, small triplets figure to win *if* they contain one of the wild cards. When you don't hold one of the wild cards, be wary of any holding less than three aces or kings.

One-eyed jacks wild doesn't work too well in stud forms. With only two wild cards available, the players tend to drop as soon as an opponent catches one up.

OPTION POKER
See Substitution Poker and Take It or Leave It.

PASS AND OUT
Sometimes called Bet or Drop, this game is similar to Jacks. There are no opening requirements, and the player under the gun must either bet or get out. No checking is allowed before the draw, and the players who have "passed out" cannot get back in by calling another player's opening bet. Thus, positional jockeying and sandbagging are out, but pure percentage play becomes more reliable.

The winning hands and staying requirements are pretty close to Jacks. The play of two pairs, triplets, and so on are the same. You can, however, relax your opening requirements a notch when you are third or so to speak because you can't be sandbagged by the players who have passed out in front of you.

PASS THE TRASH
See Anaconda.

PEDRO
See Mexican Stud.

PEEP AND TURN
See Mexican Stud.

PIG–IN–THE–POKE
See Wild Widow.

PIP POKER
A game in which point counting entirely replaces the rank of poker hands. Aces count 1. Court cards count 10. All pip cards count their face value. Usually dealt in the form of draw poker, the game can be played high, low, or both ways.

Pip Poker is not popular enough, and is not taken seriously enough, to justify a complete set of odds. But here's the probability of catching a pat 50 on the first five cards:

$$P = \frac{\left(\dfrac{16 \cdot 15 \cdot 14 \cdot 13 \cdot 12}{5!}\right)}{\left(\dfrac{52 \cdot 51 \cdot 50 \cdot 49 \cdot 48}{5!}\right)} = 0.0017$$

which is a little less than the probability of catching a pat flush—so take it from there.

In a variation called Red and Black, red cards have a positive value and black cards have a negative value. In other words, a black king nullifies a red king. When played low, or high-low, black court cards are very valuable and the hands sometimes end up on the negative side of zero!

PISTOL STUD

This game is exactly like Five-Card Stud except that the first betting interval takes place after the players receive their hole card. Thus, pistol stud merely adds another betting interval.

The staying requirements are simple: a high card. But if Pistol Stud is dealt frequently in your group, it is sound strategy to make an occasional loose call on an 8 or a 9. When analyzing a tight opponent's play, you can be pretty sure that a small up card did not pair his hole card if he called a sizable bet at the outset, and you can also be pretty sure that a high up card will pair his hole card about 20 percent of the time.

Remember that an ace-high (no pair) will hold up in Pistol Stud more often than in regular Five-Card Stud, simply because many players drop potential small pairs before the first up card is dealt.

PROCTER AND GAMBLE

A widow game. Each player receives four down cards. Then three cards are turned up, one at the time, in the widow. The last widow card and all like it are wild. Because everybody has at least one wild card, the winning hands run high. Don't get excited about any holding less than four-of-a-kind. Unless you hold high triplets from the outset, it's a gamble to play Procter and Gamble. Anything can happen on the last turn.

PROGRESSIVE JACKS

The mechanics of the deal and the basic strategy for this game are identical to Jacks. The opening requirements vary, however, if the pot is not opened on the first round. On the second round (following a new deal and usually an additional ante), it takes queens or better to open. On the third round, kings or better. On the fourth round, aces or better. Then back to kings . . . and on back down to jacks.

Normally, the staying requirements for Jacks will apply to Progressive Jacks. Obviously, though, a pair of kings becomes a short pair if aces are required to open. Even so, short pairs are often worth a call in fixed-limit sessions when the ante is repeated with each progression; if the opening requirements have gone up to aces or better and then start back down, even inside straights are worth a gamble.

PUSH

Here's a high-low game from Irv Roddy's *Friday Night Poker*. First, each player receives a hole card. Then the player on the dealer's left gets an up card. He either keeps it or pushes it to the player on his left. If he pushes, he gets as a replacement the top card off the deck and must keep it for the time being.

The next player may accept the card pushed to him, or he may push it along and replace it with an up card off the deck. And so on. When the dealer pushes, the card is burned.

The first betting interval takes place after everyone has an up card. Then the second up card is dealt, and the active players can keep both up cards or push *either* one of them! The second betting interval occurs when every active player has received his second up card. And so on until every active player has four up cards.

Then each active player is allowed to buy one substitution card, either up or down, depending on how he shucks. Final betting interval. Showdown.

Push sounds like fun, but I haven't played it enough to offer much advice. Here's part of what Roddy said:

"As in most high-low games, you should tend to prefer a low start rather than a high start. The ideal situation is to be playing low and have a high player to your right. The reverse is also good. In short, if you are not competing with the player who must push to you, he will sometimes 'fatten you.'

"One of the difficult problems that constantly arises in this game is the treatment of an 8. On the first and second up cards, I recommend pushing it. An 8 doesn't win the low often enough. On the third and fourth push you must decide on the basis of the apparent strength of the other low opponents and the exposed cards. If you are holding ace down and 2, 5, 8 up and receive a 6, but the 4's and 3's are all dead, you should hold the 8. You can only improve to a 7-6-5, and that isn't much of an improvement. On the other hand, if a preponderance of the pictures has been exposed so that the 3's and 4's are live and there is some strong low competition, push the 8."

RACEHORSE
See Blind Stud.

RED AND BLACK
See Pip Poker.

REMBRANDT
In this draw game, all face cards are wild! But Rembrandt is not as outrageous as it might seem on first thought. There are only 12 face cards—which is exactly the same number of cards that are wild in Dr. Pepper. Indeed, the playing requirements and strategy set forth under the entry for Dr. Pepper draw and stud will also apply to Rembrandt. There is a slight difference, however. In Rembrandt, five 10's have the same value as five kings have in Dr. Pepper; five 9's, five queens; and so on. As in Dr. Pepper, the only real powerhouse is five aces.

REPLACEMENT
See Substitution Poker.

RICKEY DE LAET
See Shifting Sands.

ROUND THE WORLD
This widow game is dealt and played like Cincinnati except that each player receives only four down cards, and only four widow cards

are turned. Flushes are stronger than they are in Cincinnati and they figure to win in Round the World unless a pair shows in the widow. Even straights will take a lot of pots.

Round the World is a good choice for high-low poker, and those players who shoot for low will have a decided advantage (especially in the California version with cards speak) because those incidental low straights and flushes will swing successfully much more often than in ten-card games like Cincinnati, and will connect more often than in Seven-Card Stud.

SELECTO
See Take It or Leave It.

SEVEN AND TWENTY–SEVEN
Numbers games like Seven and Twenty-Seven, or Two and Twenty-Two, are not usually covered in poker books. Yet, they are played with money and cards; moreover, they are quite popular in some dealer's choice sessions, although I've heard more than one player complain, "It ain't even poker!" Poker or not, these games are suited for bluffery and strategical betting and positional play.

In Seven and Twenty-Seven, each player receives one down card and one up card. The object of the game is to get closer to seven or twenty-seven than your opponents. Aces count either 1 or 11—or both. Court cards count ½. Pip cards count their face value, from 2 through 10. Thus, K-6 adds up to 6½, and A-7 adds up to either 8 or 18.

The first betting interval occurs after the first two cards have been dealt. Then each active player can hold or receive another up card. A betting interval follows each round of up cards. In most circles, a player can hold once and then hit on the next round of dealing, but cannot receive another up card after he has held twice in succession. A player who holds twice in succession is said to freeze.

Conservative players quickly fold anything except a low hand. Once convinced that they are beaten for low, they drop out instead of shooting for high (unless they don't have much competition for high). What sort of low hand one should play depends in large measure on the cards that show around the board. Generally, in a loose eight-handed game, you'll need either the nuts (perfect seven) or the half (6½ or 7½) to win. But sometimes excellent opportunities arise even on a 10-A low—if you've got the 10 in the hole, have only one or two opponents for low, and have a good position for bluffery. For example:

You hold (10)/A. All the other players show high cards (higher than 8) except a single opponent, who has (?)/Q. If your ace is the only one up, it's on you to bet. Check. If another ace shows first and bets, just call. On the deal, hold. Then bet or raise vigorously. If your opponent for low calls, hold again in front of him. At this point, just after your display of strength made first by betting after your sand-bagging play and second by freezing, your opponent will be tempted to draw for a better low hand if he is under seven or to pursue high if he is over seven. If he does freeze, however, you have to assume that he has the half and will call all the way; in this case, your proper play is to fold during the next betting interval. But if he is a very stubborn player, you may want to try him one more round.

The example above illustrates just one of the many opportunities for bluffery and positional strategy in Seven and Twenty-Seven. Moreover, the game usually builds such large pots that you can afford to speculate a few chips during the early rounds of betting. But get the hell out as soon as you see that your footwork has got you in a corner.

Problem hands occur when you have five or six and don't know whether to hold or go for the nuts. It's best to hold the first round to see what the opposition is going to do. If you do have several opponents for low, draw at the next opportunity. Then get out fast if you overshoot the low mark. The best "problem" hand occurs when you hold A-A or A-5. Draw! If you happen to end up with A-A-5, you'll have a perfect hand for both high and low. When you end up with a hand like A-A-J-4, you have the half for both high and low and will probably win one way or the other, if not both ways; sometimes such a holding will get three-fourths of the pot.

Remember that having the nuts does not necessarily mean that you will win money on the hand. When several lows tie against a single high opponent, all the lows can lose money, especially during the last betting intervals. Assume that Players A and B have perfect lows. They can make money by betting and raising as long as they have three or more opponents. When the opposition narrows down to only two opponents, they will merely break even by betting, since each will get one-fourth of the pot. The moment that A and B have only a single opponent (going high), they will lose 25 percent of every bet they make or call.

Whenever the competition for low is very stiff, remember that it's easier to make a perfect low by hitting a hand like 6-K than by hitting one like 4-2. With the 6-K, any face card will make you a perfect low, but with the 4-2 only an ace or *two* face cards will do the trick. Who would hit the half? I do, sometimes, when three or four low hands have held in front of me. Why? Well, consider a very loose quarter-limit game, with seven players who usually stay all the way or until they bust out for high. Typically, the betting gets off modestly, say 10¢. Toward the end, the betting increases to 25¢ and raises become common. Assuming that only three raises are allowed, it could cost you $1 for each betting interval. And when those high hands start hitting court cards, the betting intervals can stretch on and on. Thus, you end up putting four or five bucks into the pot and you're not certain of getting anything back. So, why not spend 10¢ during the early rounds of betting? If you hit a court card, sit back comfortably and watch the pot grow. If you bust, get out and give them your 10¢.

Also see Two and Twenty-Two.

SEVEN–CARD FLIP

Each player receives four down cards, and he turns up two. Then the game proceeds exactly like Seven-Card Stud. The playing requirements for tight sessions include triplets, a high pair, fourflushes, and bobtails. Fold two low pairs unless the betting is nominal. (See the discussion under Seven-Card Stud.)

The winning hands and strategy are pretty much the same as in Seven-Card Stud, except that full houses and triplets tend to be more concealed. Normally, it's best to keep your pairs and high cards in the hole. But watch for opportunities to misrepresent your holding. When you have ♣10-♠10-♦10-♦J, for example, you may want to turn up ♦10-♦J to make your opponents think you are shooting for a flush.

SEVEN–CARD STUD

Also called Seven-Toed Pete and Down-the-River, this is a standard stud game in which each player receives two cards down and one up before the first betting interval takes place. Then each active player receives another up card. Second betting interval. Another up card. And so on until each active player has four up cards. Then another card is dealt in the hole, and a final betting interval takes place.

Seven-Card Stud is an excellent game for analyzing your opponents' holdings, based on your knowledge of their habits, the history of the betting during the hand, and what cards show or have been folded. But the last card comes down, so it's hard to tell on the final round of betting whether you hold a lock on a flush or some such holding; your opponents can make a full house or even four-of-a-kind without a single pair showing.

The staying requirements (based on tight play) are tabulated immediately below for quick reference, and each playing hand is discussed in the paragraphs that follow the tabulation.

First Three Cards	Four Cards	Five Cards	Six Cards
1. (6-6)/6	(6-6)/6-X	(6-6)/6-X-X	(6-6)/6-X-X-X
2. (♥-♥)/♥	(♥-♥)/♥-♥	(♥-♥)/♥-♥-X	(♥-♥)/♥-♥-X-X
3. (8-9)/10	(8-9)/10-J	(8-9)/10-J-X	(8-9)/10-J-X-X
4. (A-10)/A	(A-10)/A-X	?	?
5. (7-7)/9	(7-7)/9-9	?	?

1. The first case—triplets—are worth playing all the way unless you have good reason to believe that another player holds a higher set. With triplets on the go, the probability that you will make a full house or better is 0.413; therefore triplets make not only a strong hand as such but also one that offers an excellent chance of improvement.

There are two approaches to betting triplets at the outset of a Seven-Card Stud hand. First, bet and raise vigorously to make it expensive for the flushes and straights. Second, sandbag to let the straights and flushes shape up, hoping for a killing during the latter rounds of betting if you make a full house. The complete poker player will use both methods from time to time. In general, I think it's best to slow play triplets until the fourth card falls because your hand will be easy to read if you bet too heavily during the first round.

After the fourth card falls, you'll have a better feeling for how the other hands are shaping up. You'll also have a modified figure on your chances of filling up. If, for example, your fourth card is a 10-spot and two of them already show around the board, your chances of filling up are considerably reduced, in which case you may want to bet heavily to discourage straights and flushes.

If the fifth card doesn't fill you up, by all means stay for the sixth card unless you have strong indications that you are already beaten. If the last card doesn't improve your triplets, you may be in trouble. Whether you call the end bet on the strength of your triplets depends on your analysis of the play, what cards are showing, the odds offered by the pot, and so on. Often it will depend on how high your triplets are.

By the way, the average winning hand in Seven-Card Stud is believed to be trip 8's or 9's or 10's. Exact figures would of course depend upon how tight or loose a particular group plays, especially in regard to straights and flushes.

2. Three cards to a flush are worth a call unless somebody taps in table stakes. If the fourth card helps the flush along, then play all the way unless (1) you have some indication that the flush will not hold up if you do hit it, (2) the pot ceases to offer proper odds, as will happen sometimes in pot limit or table stakes play, and (3) a large number of your flush cards show around the board. The probability of your hitting the flush with four cards to come is 0.180, but this figure will vary with the number of your flush cards that are exposed around the board.

Many players raise if their first four cards are of the same suit, and some writers recommend a raise because it's almost even money (probability = 0.472) that you'll fill the flush and it's over 2 to 1 that it will win if you do make it. A good deal depends, of course, on the cards that are showing around the table, how much strength the opposition has shown, your position, the betting limits, and so on. As a general rule, however, I can't recommend that you raise on the come, and certainly not in pot limit or table stakes, except occasionally to mix up your play and to keep the opposition guessing. My reason is that a raise will often drive out one or more players, thereby lowering the odds you are getting on your money while at the same time increasing the price you pay to shoot for the flush. In pot limit or table stakes, I think you should be guided to a degree by the odds on hitting the flush on the next up card and should not assume that you can play all the way (unless you go all in). If the fifth card doesn't fill the flush, your probability of improving is lowered to 0.350. If the sixth card doesn't help, your probability is lowered to 0.196. When a shrewd player holding triplets or even two high pairs figures out that you are playing for a flush, he could well tap after the fifth or sixth cards are up. If the pot held $50 and he tapped on the sixth card for about $100, you would not have a call.

When bucking triplets with a fourflush, figure not only the probability of making the flush but also of *winning*. The great advantage that another player has when he holds triplets over your fourflush is that he doesn't necessarily have to improve to win, and even if you do make a flush he has an almost equally good chance of filling up. Your probability of winning is the product of your probability of flushing times the probability that he will not fill up. The probability of his making a full house or better is 0.389 (when he holds triplets on the first four cards); of *not* filling up, $1 - 0.389 = 0.611$. Your probability of winning, then, is $0.472 \times 0.611 = 0.288$.

Another point is that the complete player in Seven-Card Stud, as well as in some widow games, will extract a considerable amount of money from his opponents by letting them see a card or two toward a flush before he taps them out. What risk is he taking by letting them draw for a moderate bet? The odds that the fourflush will not connect on the fourth and fifth cards are about 4 to 1.

Of course a player can't take time out to make exacting mathematical decisions at the table. But remember, in summary, that fourflushes will usually give you a good gamble in Seven-Card Stud with fixed limits, but that they will often get you into deep water in table stakes or pot limit.

3. Three cards to a straight are worth a call, especially in limit poker. If the fourth card doesn't help the hand, either by continuing the straight, making a pair, or possibly making three of a suit toward a flush, the hand should be thrown in. As Table V in Part Two, page 112, shows, three cards open on both ends are much better than a gut shot or a closed-end straight. Remember also that it's much better to have a potential high straight in case you start pairing up or run into another straight.

Betting, raising, and folding on straights in Seven-Card Stud should go pretty much the same as for flushes, and the points brought out in the paragraphs above will hold true, more or less, for straights. It is true that straights won't win quite as many pots for you; on the other hand, you'll make more of them.

4. A pair of aces or kings are worth seeing at least two more cards unless the other players indicate great strength, and providing that neither of the other two shows around the board. If one more shows, you may have a call—but beware of an open pair, which could be wired up in the hole. If you make two pairs, you'll win a lot of pots with them; but you'll also lose a lot. Whether you play two high pairs all the way should depend upon the odds offered by the pot, and on whether you think you've got the best hand. Even aces over, however, is not a very strong hand in Seven-Card Stud, and most players tend to overvalue it considerably.

5. A low pair in the hole is definitely worth a moderate call if another one doesn't show around the board. If you make triplets, you have a strong hand—and it is completely hidden from your opponents. But a small pair composed of one up card and one down card is quite another matter. The probability of making triplets remains the same, but triplets in this case would also give you an exposed pair, thereby making your hand easier to read. In tight play, I recommend that you fold a small split pair. In loose play, see another card if your kicker is a high card. In either case, follow the advice given under number 1 if you trip up on the fourth card.

If you make two small pairs on the fourth card, think twice before getting your feet too wet. Remember that only four cards in the deck will make you a full house. Remember also that two high pairs are much, much better than two low pairs—and that the medial two-pair hand is jacks over. A small two-pair hand isn't much better than a pair of aces, and offers very little chance of improvement. Consider the following example:

Your opponent holds (K-10)/K-10. You hold (4-2)/2-4. Your chances of drawing out on him are slim, because only two deuces and two fours will improve your hand as it stands. If you had held (A-2)/A-4, however, your chances of drawing out on kings up would be doubled, for eight cards—two aces, three deuces, and three fours —would improve your holding.

♥ ♥ ♥

I want to point out that the scale of winning cards varies quite a bit in Seven-Card Stud, and sometimes even a single pair of aces is worth a call on the last bet *if* you are not calling on the strength of your hand but on the weakness of your opponent's. For example, your opponent started off strong with (?-?)/J-Q, and a couple of jacks and queens showed around the board. You decide that he may be shooting for a straight. When he ends up with (?-?)/J-Q-7-6/(?), you can pretty much figure that neither the 7 nor the 6 paired his hole cards, and therefore he couldn't have two pairs (*if* he *was* playing for the straight). In such a case, you may want to call his bet, for several reasons. First, you may have a winner if he hasn't hit the straight. Second, you establish the impression that you do not have to have a lock to play and will thereby discourage the other players from trying to drive you out of the pot at every opportunity. Third, you will thoroughly confuse your opponents with such a play. But I can't recommend any player making this call unless he's had a lot of experience in card analysis. On the other hand, I want to emphasize that a pair of aces is as good as a full house—if it wins the pot!

SEVEN–CARD STUD HIGH–LOW
This one is probably the most popular dealer's choice game in the United States at present. It is dealt exactly like Seven-Card Stud. The big difference is that the lowest hand wins half the pot.

As stated in Chapter 7, the cardinal rule for winning play in most (but not quite all) high-low games is to play for low, especially in cards speak and the California scale. This rule, if followed to the letter, will save you a good deal of money if your group frequently deals Seven-Card Stud High-Low, a game in which enough cards are dealt to make low straights and flushes easier to hit than in five- or six-cards games like Sudden Death, but not enough cards to make full houses as common as in ten-card games like Cincinnati. This, then, is the swinger's game.

The conservative playing requirements are tabulated below for easy reference and comparison, and the hands are explained more fully in the paragraphs that follow the tabulation. Note that a few hands are playable in a particular method of declaration but maybe not in another method. Also see Tables V and VI in Part Two, pages 112–113.

HANDS TO PLAY ON FIRST THREE CARDS

You Hold	Method of Declaration		
	Cards Speak	Chips	Consecutive
1. (2-3)/4	play	play	play
2. (2-K)/4	play	play	play
3. (A-A)/A	play	play	play
4. (K-K)/K	FOLD	play	play
5. (A-A)/2	play	play	play
6. (A-A)/Q	fold	fold	fold
7. (7-8)/9	play	fold	fold
8. (♦7♦8)/♦K	?	fold	fold

1. Three cards to a perfect low make the best hand to start with. An ace is a mighty good card to hold, for reasons explained below, but my favorite sequence is 3-4-5 (for the California scale) because it is open on both ends for straightening. Of course, any three cards to a 7 or lower are playable. If you help your low hand on the fourth card, you are in good shape with three more cards to come. When you don't further your low hand on the fourth card, stay for the fifth unless the board looks very low and the betting is stiff. If neither the fourth nor fifth card helps your low hand, it is best to bow out unless you see that the whole board is painted or paired. And figure the players as well as the board. For example:

You hold (2-3)/4-10-J. Opponent A holds (?-?)/Q-2-2. Opponent B holds (?-?)/A-6-K. Opponent C holds (?-?)/8-8-Q. The other players have folded. If C bets his open pair of 8's, he probably has help for high. Opponent A has either busted his low hand or helped a high hand. Opponent B could be drawing to a 6-low. Think back to the previous round of betting. Did B come out betting on his A-6? If he didn't, the 6 could have paired him. Did he look at his hole cards when the 6 fell? How many 6's and aces have been folded?

In any event, you have a lock on low as it now stands, so call all bets. You can still make a very good low hand, or you could possibly win with the J-10. But if opponent B catches another low card on the next deal, you'll have to credit him with a very good low hand or a one-card draw to one. Fold unless you also have a good draw at that point (and fold anyway if a large bet is made in pot limit or table stakes). If you catch a 5 and he catches a 7, play. But if you catch the 7 and he catches the 5, fold unless the betting is modest. In other words, don't draw against a hand that you can't beat even by filling your best possible low hand.

2. Play on any two low cards (except possibly a 7-6) unless the betting and raising make it too expensive. If the next up card furthers the low hand, see the fifth card and follow the advice given under 1.

3. Trip aces are worth a play. When you fill up, you almost surely have a winner for high. You can also end up with a good low hand along with three aces for high. In cases where you have only two or three opponents, a hand like (A-A)/A-2-5-9/(10) will sometimes swing in cards speak.

4. Fold three kings or any set of triplets except aces in cards speak. As explained in Chapter 7, high triplets cannot win low (except on very rare occasions), and the high money alone doesn't justify your playing against all those little bobtails and fourflush-lows. The only exception in cards speak is in a loose game with seven players who stay all the way; you'll often have to fill up to win in such loose play, but you'll make some money when you do win.

In chips or consecutive declaration, high triplets are sometimes worth a gamble if they are well concealed. The object here is to make a full house and slow play it. Then, if a player with a very good low hand drives out the rest of the players, let him swing into you with his Little Minnie or low flush. When he does swing into your full house, you'll get all the money because he must win both ways to win either way. Your alternate strategy is to raise when you have four or five active opponents, if you are in position to build the pot by so raising. If you don't improve your triplets, raise on the last card to indicate strength *if* you think that such a raise would convince the possible swingers to go only for low money.

Triplets lower than 8's are worth a call in chips declare. Sometimes you'll end up with what looks like a very good low hand, thereby convincing your opponents to declare high. Thus, you can sometimes win all the money with a small full house. In consecutive declaration, however, watch your position carefully on the latter rounds of betting. If at all possible, you'll want to be the last to declare so that you can surprise everyone with your low full house. Position is so important when you hold a hand like (2-2)/2-3-4-7/(4) that all your latter round bets, calls, and raises should be purely positional. Try to keep the players in or drive them out to your positional advantage.

For example, player A, on your left, is high with (?-?)/A-K-5-8/(?). Player B, on your right, holds (?-?)/A-Q-4-8/(?). Player A checks. Player B checks. If you bet, you will have to declare first, and if you go high either A or B, or both, may go low. But if the hand is checked out, A will have to declare first. He may go high if he has figured you and B for low hands. Player B may also go high, especially if he has paired up a couple of times. So, you have a chance to win all the pot by checking along and thereby retaining your ideal position.

Consider another example in which you make a positional raise on six cards. You hold (2-2)/2-3-4-6. Player A, on your right, is high with (?-?)/♣A-K-7-4. Player B, on your left, holds (?-?)/A-Q-7-6. Player A bets. You raise the limit, hoping to drive out player B. If you don't drive B out, you'll be sandwiched on the declaration and won't have much chance to win all the pot. Why should B drop in such a good position? Because he figures A for a flush high and possibly a shot at a seventy-four low. Since you raised, he will figure you for a 6-low and possibly a straight. Your raise should also convince player A that you hold a very good low hand, and he isn't likely to swing even if he does have the 7-low. Assuming that you do succeed in driving player B out, you can probably win at least half the pot no matter what you catch. Player A will probably declare high (whether he has the flush or not!) and you can contest him if you fill up. If you don't fill up, declare low and take half the pot. Should he perchance declare low, then you go high, unless you happen to make the 6-low, in which case you contest him.

But remember that too much fancy footwork will just cost you a lot of money in low-limit sessions with loose, inexperienced players.

5. Two low cards with a pair are worth a call, especially if the pair is aces. Play as long as your low hand continues to develop. If you make two pairs, aces over, play along in cards speak if the betting isn't too rough. When you have what looks like a good low hand on six cards, raise to drive out some of the players. Such a hand would be (A-2)/A-2-3-4. Your aces over may win high and you have a good shot at low. Even if you catch a 9 or 10, you can still win all the money in cards speak. Therefore, consider the board carefully when

you hold aces over with a mediocre low hand. An example will illustrate what can happen.

You hold (A-2)/A-2-3-6/(10). Player A has (?-?)/6-6-J-A/(?). He bets. You raise the maximum limit. In pot limit, bet all you can. In table stakes, tap. You have nothing to lose, unless he has flush cards showing. If you'll consider A's hand carefully, you'll see that you have him locked *one way or the other* and could win all the money. If he has a 6 low, you win high with two pairs. If he has a full house, or the case 6 in the hole, you win low with your 10-6. If he has a pair of aces along with his 6's, you win *low* with your aces over, since his best low hand would be a jack. If he has jacks over (or has another pair in the hole), you win both high and low! In this particular example, the only way you could lose money by tapping is when he holds a concealed flush along with a good low hand. So be careful if three of his up cards are in suit. Of course he could have a flush when only two of his up cards are in suit, but that's a gamble worth taking unless he has tipped a fourflush in one way or another. The timid of purse will say, "But why hazard a tap when the chances are pretty slim that you'll win *all* the pot?" Well, there is a chance that you will win all the pot with your cards and there is another chance that you will drive him out with your tap. It's also a good strategic play for the long haul. The fact that you tapped (or raised the maximum limit) on a hand that wasn't very high or very low will confuse the opposition and get you a lot of calls in the future.

6. Fold a high card and a low pair. You would have to hit four little cards to have a good low hand, and it's futile to pursue high, for reasons explained above and in Chapter 7.

7. Play a middling straight only in cards speak. You could win both ways if your opponents start pairing up. In chips declare or consecutive declaration, you'll probably have a winner one way or the other when you end up with a 9-high straight and a 9-low—but often you'll be guessing which way!

8. Three cards to a flush along with two low kickers are worth a call in cards speak. Again, you could win both ways. But, again, you'll often be guessing which way in chips declare or consecutive declaration. My own rule, which I sometimes break in low-limit play, is to stay on flushes only if my first three suit cards are all low or contain an ace and a low card.

♥ ♥ ♥

If the joker is used as a wild card or as the bug in Seven-Card Stud High-Low, remember that anyone who holds it has a much better chance of making a swing hand. Also, it's a little easier for an opponent to make a good low hand. So, tighten up your play somewhat if you don't hold the joker, and tighten up considerably if it shows in an opponent's hand.

Sometimes wild cards are designated in Seven-Card Stud High-Low. Usually they will be high cards, such as jacks. The staying requirements are stiff. At the outset, play only three cards to a perfect low, preferably with one of the wild cards working for you. Play high only if you hold two wild cards, or one wild card along with two natural aces; in either case, you have a chance of making a perfect low as well as a good high hand.

When playing with wild cards, beware of a sixty-five low. Beware of any high hand less than aces full.

SEVEN–TOED PETE
See Seven-Card Stud.

SHIFTING SANDS
This variation of Mexican Stud is also called Rickey de Laet. Personally, I call it Decatur Disaster! Once I drove down from Tennessee to pick up some easy money in a very loose table stakes game that was being floated in and around Decatur, Alabama. Shifting Sands was a popular game among this group, but I had never played it before. After tangling in several pots, I drove back to Tennessee talking to myself.

The mechanics of the deal are exactly the same as for Mexican Stud, which in turn is nothing but Five-Card Stud in which every card is dealt down and each player rolls his up card. The major feature of Shifting Sands is that your hole card, and all like it in your hand, is wild! Since you select your hole card on each round, your wild card can change from round to round.

In The Complete Guide to Winning Poker, Albert H. Morehead says that this game is so wild that the only conservative strategy is to fold unless you hold a pair wired. That's what I thought, too—until I tangled with that bunch in Decatur.

Actually, a pair back to back is a big trap in high stakes play unless you learn how to bet them. My reasoning is difficult to explain, so

I'll recount my Decatur experiences to illustrate it. As Morehead suggested, I anted along until I held a pair back to back. Then I rolled one and sandbagged, confident that I had the best of the game with two wild cards. When my third card was an ace or a king, I rejoiced because then I held high triplets and often had a lock on the board as it stood. Then, on the fourth card, the sands shifted on me. Invariably I would bet out, and just as invariably one of the players around the board would tap.

After analyzing their hands, I would decide, before I folded, that they had cinched a flush or a straight. Indeed, a flush or a straight won a large percentage of the pots. Typically, these flushes and straights were made with only one wild card working. Here's the odd thing: You can make a flush or a straight quicker with one wild card than with two! Let's play a hand to see how it works.

The first of seven players holds A-10. He rolls the ace and bets. The second player calls on ♦8-9. The third player folds 2-7. The fourth calls on 4-4. The fifth calls on J-Q. The sixth folds K-5. The seventh calls on ♥A-6.

Here's a table of the active players and their holdings:

Player 1	Player 2	Player 4	Player 5	Player 7
(10)/A	(♦8)/9	(4)/4	(J)/Q	(♥A)/6

On the next card, player 1 catches a king and bets. Player 2 catches an off-suit trey and calls. Player 4 catches a jack and calls. Player 5 catches a 10 and calls. Player 7 catches an off-suit queen and folds. So, our table becomes:

Player 1	Player 2	Player 4	Player 5
(10)/A-K	(3)/♦8-9	(4)/4-J	(10)/J-Q

On the next round, player 1 catches a 5 and checks. Player 2 catches a deuce and checks along. Player 4 catches an 8 and bets on his three jacks. Player 5 catches an ace and taps. Players 1 and 2 fold. What does player 4 do with his two wild cards? Well, here are the hands:

Player 4	Player 5
(4)/4-J-8	(J)/Q-10-A

Note that player 5 already has a straight made—no matter what he catches on the fifth card. If he catches a deuce, for instance, he turns up the jack and uses the deuce as his wild card. If he catches another ace, he turns up the jack and uses the ace wild in his straight. But player 4 doesn't have a straight made even though he now holds two wild cards and two cards to a straight! To draw out on player 5, he must catch another 4, a jack, or an 8. (A queen, 7, 10, or 9 would make a straight, but in this case it wouldn't beat player 5's higher straight.) If both players' stacks contain a lot of money, player 4's proper play is to fold after the tap—and drive home talking to himself!

Several times during that Decatur session I found myself in player 4's position: beaten by a straight or a flush on four cards. On my way back to Tennessee, I decided that I should have tapped with my two wild cards *before* those four-card straights and flushes could shape up. I never did go back to Decatur and therefore didn't face the cold reality of tapping at the poker table. I have, however, dealt the game in limit poker. My conclusion is that wired pairs are not the power-houses that I at first thought they were. The trouble with the wired pair is that it's too difficult to improve. It's exactly as hard to make four-of-a-kind in Shifting Sands as it is to make two pairs or triplets (with your hole card figured in on the pairs) in ordinary Five-Card Stud. I'll play a wired pair in Shifting Sands for low limits, but I'd rather have 10-J of the same suit. If I had a choice on three cards in a loose limit game, I would choose ♣10-J-Q every time over 2-2-A! With 2-2-A, only five cards would improve the hand on the next round (three aces and two deuces), whereas 22 cards to ♣10-J-Q would make a straight or better.

Another side of the argument, however, is that the 2-2-A doesn't necessarily have to improve to win. True. But in loose games with lots of active players, a flush or a straight will win the majority of pots. I pitted the ♣10-J-Q against the ♦2-♠2-♥A and dealt out a hundred hands. The wired pair won 39 times; the possible straight flush, 61 times!

Whatever cards you decide to play in Shifting Sands, be very careful when rolling your hole card. Mistakes can be costly.

♥ ♥ ♥

A similar game is also called Shifting Sands. In this variation, the first up card and all like it in your hand are wild. The game is a little easier to play because your wild card—and your opponents'—is fixed early in the play instead of shifting on each round. In this variation, it is almost impossible to cinch straights and flushes on four cards. Consequently, a wired pair is a much better holding than in the hole-card-wild version.

SHOTGUN

This one is a draw game with additional betting intervals. First, each player receives three cards face down. A betting interval follows. Another down card. Another betting interval. Another (fifth) down card. Another betting interval. Then each player can draw to his hand. Another betting interval. Showdown. Generally, the winning hands run slightly lower than in Jacks. There is less action on straights and flushes because the increase in betting intervals, and the fact that you start betting on only three cards, makes it too expensive to shoot for them. The staying requirements (conservative) for the first three cards include (1) a high pair and (2) *high* cards to a straight or flush. In the first case, play your high pair all the way unless you have reason to believe that it is beaten. In the second case, fold after the next down card has been dealt if it does not continue your flush or straight and does not make a high pair.

Shotgun is sometimes played high-low. Generally, it is best to play for low, as in most other high-low games. But see the discussion under High-Low Draw.

SHOVE 'EM ALONG

See Take It or Leave It.

SHOWDOWN

A poker hand played for the ante only, without additional bets or raises. It is almost a pure gamble. Except for carding knowledge in draw or substitution forms, the expert has no advantage over the poor player. Any dealer's choice game can be put on a Showdown basis, but Beat Your Neighbor is the most popular form.

SHOW FIVE CARDS

Here's a roll 'em back number from *Poker: The Nation's Most Fascinating Card Game:* "Seven cards are dealt face down to each player, and each player looks at his cards. At a signal from the dealer, each player turns up one of his cards on the table. Before giving the signal, the dealer should inquire whether everyone is ready. After the cards are exposed, there is a round of betting. After the betting is completed, the dealer gives the signal for the exposure of the second cards. All these second cards must be exposed at the same time. The process continues until each player in the game has five cards exposed for the showdown. The game is usually played high-low. It is not unusual for a player to change his mind during the game and try for low rather than high."

Although medium-sized triplets figure to win in Seven-Card Stud, they make a doubtful calling hand in Show Five. The reason is that too many straights and flushes are filled on hands that would not be played in Seven-Card Stud. In Show Five High-Low, proceed cautiously on any low hand worse than a seventy-five.

SHUCK 'EM

See Substitution and Little Squeeze.

SIX–CARD STUD

This game is like Five-Card Stud with an additional card and betting interval on the end. The sixth card comes up in some groups, down in others. In still another variation, the fifth card comes down and the sixth one up.

The staying requirements are the same as for Five-Card Stud. (Play straights and flushes only incidentally to good high cards.) In a loose game, the average winning hand is two pairs, but a single pair of aces or kings will often hold up in tighter play.

Six-Card Stud is not quite as unpredictable as Sudden Death when played low. When played high-low, it is best to stay only on hands that have swing potential. But straights and flushes are difficult to hit in Six-Card Stud, so the ace becomes the key card. If you pair the ace, you have a good high hand and still have low possibilities. When you make two pairs, aces over, you can win both ways against a single opponent if he also makes two pairs. When you make and get clobbered on a fairly good low hand against one or two opponents, your ace will sometimes pull you through for high money in cards speak. The ace is such a valuable card that extremely cautious players will not stay in without one! In most circles, however, you can loosen up a bit and play on any two cards to a 7 low; an ace and an 8 (or lower); and a pair of aces. But fold any other pair in Six-Card Stud High-Low.

SOUTHERN CROSS

In this variation of Cincinnati, the widow contains nine cards arranged in the shape of a cross, such as

Q
7
A 10 2 6 K
6
K

Each player may use cards from either row, but not from both rows; that is, A-10-2-6-K or Q-7-2-6-K. The widow cards are turned up either clockwise or counterclockwise. The center card is turned up last. In some high-low circles, players can use one row for high and the other row for low.

Winning hands run a little higher than in Cincinnati. The playing requirements are stiffer, mainly because Southern Cross has almost twice as many betting intervals as Cincinnati has.

In another variation, only five cards are turned up in the center, such as

7
A 2 K
6

Again, each player may use cards from either row, but not from both rows. Winning hands run lower in this variation than in Cincinnati. The big difference is that flushes hold up more often for high, and sometimes even straights will swing in high-low.

SPECIAL HANDS

Dutch Straight. Also called Alternate Straight, Kilter, or Skip Straight. It is a sequence of odd or even cards separated by one rank, such as 6-8-10-Q-A or 5-7-9-J-K. A Dutch Straight beats triplets but loses to regular straights.

Round-the-Corner Straight. A "circular" sequence that contains both high cards and low cards, such as 4-3-2-A-K or 3-2-A-K-Q. It beats triplets but loses to Dutch Straights and regular straights.

Fourflush. Any four cards in suit. Beats single pairs, loses to two pairs. In some circles, a fourflush with a pair beats one without a pair; that is, ♣K-♦K-♦A-♦3-♦6 beats Q-♦K-♦A-♦3-♦6. Also see New York Stud.

Blaze. Five court cards. Beats two pairs, loses to triplets. Since this hand is made up of jacks, queens, and kings, each Blaze also contains two pairs. The higher two pairs win in case two blazes tangle for a pot.

Big Tiger. Also called Big Cat. It consists of a king high and an 8 low with no pair, such as K-J-10-9-8 or K-Q-J-10-8. Beats straights, loses to flushes.

Little Tiger. Also called Little Cat. It consists of an 8 high and a trey low with no pair, such as 8-7-6-5-3. Beats straights, loses to Big Tigers.

Big Dog. Ace high, 9 low, with no pair. Beats straights, loses to Little Tigers.

Little Dog. 7 high, deuce low, with no pair. Beats straights, loses to Big Dogs.

Woolworth. 10 high, 5 low, with no pair. Beats triplets, loses to straights.

Skeet. Also called Pelter. It consists of a 9, a 5, and a deuce, with one card between the 9 and the 5 and another card between the 5 and the deuce, such as 9-7-5-3-2. Beats triplets, loses to straights. A Skeet in suit has a higher value, beating four-of-a-kind in some groups and straight flushes in others.

Big Bobtail. A four-card straight in suit, such as ♠6-7-8-9. Beats full houses, loses to four-of-a-kind.

Flash. The joker with a club, a diamond, a heart, and a spade. Beats two pairs, loses to triplets.

Double-Ace Flush. In some poker circles that play jokers and wild cards, a flush with two aces beats an A-K flush.

♥   ♥   ♥

There is some conflict between the Special Hands as to what beats what. There are too many of them! Most groups that play Special Hands at all limit them to certain hands or groups of hands; thus, Skeets, Dutch Straights, Flashes, and so on are not usually recognized in groups that play Dogs and Cats. So, you don't have to remember all the Special Hands in a typical dealer's choice session.

In addition to Special Hands, some groups play bonuses (also called premiums, penalties, and royalties) on such very good hands as natural straight flushes in high poker and wheels in low poker. The player holding such a powerhouse collects, in addition to the pot, a predetermined sum from each player at the table.

SPIT–IN–THE–OCEAN

One of the earlier widow games, Spit usually gets a lot of action at the table because every player has at least one wild card on the go. The game is dealt like draw poker except that each player receives only four down cards. The fifth card is dealt face up in the center, is wild, and is common to all players. Usually, the widow card and *all like it* are wild. Thus, if you hold 4-4-X-X and a four-spot turns up in the widow, you have three wild cards.

The following tabulations and text for playing requirements are based on a conservative game:

Hands to Play

You Hold	Wild Widow
1. (4-X-X-X)	4 (for example)
2. (4-K-K-X)	Same
3. (Q-Q-6-6)	Same
4. (A-A-X-X)	Same
5. (♥9-10-J-Q)	Same

Traps to Avoid

6. (♥9-10-J-X)	Same
7. (10-J-Q-K)	Same
8. (♣-♣-♣-♣)	Same

1. A wild card among your four draw cards is worth a call if it isn't too expensive. Usually, you should draw three cards and not hold a kicker. If you hit any pair, you'll have four-of-a-kind (the

pair plus the wild widow plus the wild card in your hand). Four-of-a-kind figures to win over the long run, especially if they are 10's or higher.

Remember, however, that winning hands vary widely in this game, and that four-of-a-kind will sometimes lose. Actually, the strength of four-of-a-kind depends largely on how many wild cards you hold. Obviously 5-6-widow-widow is a much better holding than 6-6-6-5 because the more wild cards you hold, the slimmer the other players' chances.

When you hold two wild cards going in, raise if you are in a good position to build the pot. When your position is bad, however, and your raise would tend to drive players out before they invested in the pot, you may choose to sandbag.

2. A wild card and a pair among your four down cards gives you four-of-a-kind at the outset. The hand may win without improvement, especially if the natural pair is jacks or higher. Remember that it's difficult to improve this hand, since only two of your paired cards and only two wild cards are left in the deck—and you must assume that all the wild cards are out if several players are active in the pot.

Although small sets of fours aren't powerhouses after the draw, I recommend that you raise on them before the draw if you are in good position to drive out some of the players. When you do succeed in driving out all but one or two opponents, play pat occasionally to discourage betting after the draw. My reasoning is that you aren't likely to improve by drawing, and that by raising and playing pat you are leading your opponents to figure you for a straight flush or five-of-a-kind. In short, playing small sets of fours is marginal—but if you do play them, play them strategically. And be quick to throw away the small pair and draw to the wild card whenever the carding indicates that small fours are already beaten.

3. Two pairs in your hand are sometimes worth a call, if they are jacks over or higher. This holding, of course, gives you a full house. But a full house will lose a lot of pots. My advice is to call on a high full house if the betting isn't too expensive. Play it pat unless the carding indicates that you are holding a loser, in which case you throw away the smaller pair, draw two, and hope to make four-of-a-kind or better.

The intrinsic weakness of this hand is that you don't hold any of the wild cards, which leaves them available for the other players. For this reason, I recommend that you throw in any full house that doesn't give you the option to draw two cards for four jacks or better. Such an option doesn't mean much, however, unless you have good carding position.

4. A pair of aces or kings are worth a call if the betting is moderate. You'll have to improve, though, before you can call an end bet. Again, a major disadvantage of this hand is that you don't hold any wild cards.

5. Play a pat straight flush vigorously, especially in limit poker. In table stakes, however, remember that five-of-a-kind is not uncommon in Spit.

6. Unless the pot offers very good odds, a possible straight flush is not worth a call. Even if the straight flush is open on both ends, only four natural cards (in addition to the remaining wild cards, if any) will fill it. But most players will make this draw at whatever odds, and many will be sucked into calling an end bet when they fill only a flush or a straight.

7 and 8. Fold a pat straight or a pat flush at the outset. It may be a winner going in, but it won't often survive the draw in loose games. Why call an opening bet, stand pat, and then be embarrassed by folding a pat hand when the betting gets rough after the draw?

STORMY WEATHER

I've decided to quote this one from *The Complete Guide to Winning Poker* not only because Morehead gives an adequate description of the game but also because he backs up a point I have made about the importance of "overlays" in widow poker. Here's Morehead's text:

"The dealer gives each player four cards, one at a time, face down; and after each of the first three rounds of cards, he deals one card face down to the center of the table, so that there is a widow of three cards. There is a betting interval, beginning with the player at the dealer's left, and with nothing required to open; then each active player may discard any part of his hand and draw cards to replace it, up to the full four cards. After the draw the dealer turns up one card in the center of the table, and there is a betting interval; a second card, and another betting interval; the third card, and the final betting interval. Each active player may select *one* of the three cards in the center to be his fifth card in the showdown.

"How to play: If there were no draw, hand-values in this game would be slightly higher than in Seven-Card Stud. However, *with* the draw before the center cards are exposed, the chances of very good hands being made are greatly increased. A flush should not be given too much faith as a winning hand, and for that reason an attempt to make a flush is usually a losing play. The best strategy is to keep high pairs in the hope of making high triplets. This holding can be turned into either four-of-a-kind or a high full house with the help of a favorable card in the widow.

"Once again, it is important to compare the value of your hand with the ranks of the up cards. Suppose you hold ♣A-♣Q-♦Q-♦8. You play before the draw and take two cards (keeping the pair of queens). After the draw you hold ♥Q-♦Q-♣Q-♠6. You have a strong hand and should usually raise at this point. Suppose you raise and two other players call. The first card of the widow proves to be the ♠K. You should now drop if another player makes a significant bet! The odds greatly favor that some other player will now hold a better hand."

STRAIGHT DRAW

Sometimes called Guts to Open, this game is the same as Jacks except that there are no minimum opening requirements at all. The average winning hands and proper staying requirements are about the same. The only difference in strategy is that you can't assume that the opener has at least jacks, especially if he opened in a late position. Here are the opening requirements necessary to give you a mathematical advantage:

Players Yet to Speak	Minimum Opening Requirements
6 or 7	Aces (or K-K with A)
5	Kings (or Q-Q with A-K)
4	Queens
3	Jacks
2	Tens, nines, eights
1	Any pair

But these figures are based on the assumption that you are not playing with a bunch of sandbaggers. In most "check and raise" or "pass and back in" sessions with six or seven players, it is not wise to open on anything less than queens in the latter positions. Generally, there is more sandbagging in Straight Draw than in Jacks. There also tends to be more calls on short pairs, fourflushes, and bobtails.

Several draw games, such as Blind Tiger, are also called Straight Draw. If ever in doubt, ask the dealer to explain his game.

STRAIGHT POKER

Each player receives five cards down. There is no draw, and only one betting interval. This game was probably the original form of poker, but it is seldom (if ever) played today.

STRIP POKER

This one has been summed up pretty well in *Esquire's Book of Gambling*:

"This fascinating variation can be played by two or . . .

"That is, to begin with you . . .

"Well, frankly, gentlemen, if you by some chance don't know how to play strip poker, this is no place to find out. The best method is to find some young lady who does know how and have her teach you.

"It simply isn't as graphic in a book."

STUD

Stud is a form of poker in which each player receives both up cards and one or more down cards, or hole cards. The various stud games, such as Five- and Seven-Card Stud, are discussed in their alphabetical places.

Conservative stud players of today, who complain about wild cards and the chimerical dealer's choice games, will be surprised to learn that stud itself was, not too long ago, a radical innovation; in fact, Robert F. Foster dismissed stud as a novelty game in his *Practical Poker*, 1905.

Stud considerably livened up poker, because it offered variety and more betting intervals than draw poker. There are several stories and

theories about the origin of stud, but no one knows for sure when
or where or how the game got its start. It was probably during the
War Between the States, or shortly thereafter.

SUBSTITUTION POKER

Sometimes called Shuck 'em, Replacement, Option Poker, and
possibly other names, this is not a specific game but a method of
adding a draw element to stud forms. Little Squeeze, for example,
is played like Five-Card Stud High-Low except that each active
player has an option to discard and draw on the end. Whether your
draw card comes up or down depends on whether you discarded an
up card or a down card. In some circles, the active players can draw
(or substitute, or replace) up to three times, as specified by the
dealer. Each substitution usually costs a fixed fee, and a betting interval follows each round.

The more common substitution games are Little Squeeze and
Six-Card Stud High-Low, but the principle is used in seven-card
forms and even two-card forms, such as Hurricane.

Position is very important in almost all forms of substitution, and
especially in high-low. The dealer has the best position because he
knows how many players have taken a substitution card before he
has to decide on whether or not to substitute. Thus, he saves money
by holding pat when he has a lock, and, more important, he often
doesn't have to risk busting a lock for low. For example, the dealer
holds (K)/A-2-7-6-J in Six-Card Stud High-Low with one substitution. Player A, on the dealer's left, shows (?)/Q-2-5-10-5; he discards the deuce (probably trying to improve two pairs or trip 5's)
and catches a 10. Player B shows (?)/4-6-3-3-Q; he discards the
queen (either going for low or drawing to trip treys) and catches a
king. Whatever B was playing doesn't matter now to the dealer
because he is in the driver's seat. The best possible low hand that
player A could have would be a queen, and the best possible low
hand that player B could have would be a king. So, the dealer holds
pat on his jack low.

If the dealer—let's call him player C now—had had to make his
decision before player B, he would be in a bind. He would have to
decide whether B was playing high or low, and would probably have
to put him on low. If B did have a low card in the hole, he would

draw one and have an excellent chance of beating C's jack. Player C therefore decides to draw, hoping to make a seventy-six. He catches a deuce, which pairs him. Player B discards the queen and catches an ace. Player A bets. Player C folds, since his best low hand is now a king. Player B raises. At the showdown, B has trip treys. Player A has two pairs, queens over. So, B wins high money *and* low money, since a pair of treys beats a pair of 5's (remember that it's six-card poker). About this time player C starts jumping up and down, swearing never to play Substitution again. Perhaps he shouldn't —except when he's dealing!

As the example above illustrates, substitution is clearly a dealer's game. But the dealer's advantage decreases as the number of cards and the number of permissible substitutions increase.

In Seven-Card Stud High-Low, substitution makes for better hands, both high and low. Therefore, tighten up somewhat on the initial staying requirements. An 8 should not be considered as a winning low card during the early rounds.

In Six-Card Stud High-Low (sometimes called Big Squeeze), your position has a bearing on the minimum staying requirements for low. In a favorable position, stay on any two cards to an 8 and even a concealed 9 if you have a wheel card up. In a bad position, play two cards to a 7, but fold if the third doesn't help the low hand. For high, play a pair of aces or any pair *lower* than 8's, but fold a pair of 8's, 9's, 10's, jacks, queens, and kings because they cannot develop into strong low hands. Fold potential straights and flushes unless they are made up of low cards. But if you want to loosen up your game, play a pair of kings, which will have a fair chance for high money if you make two pairs, and a pair of 8's, which could develop into a middling low or could improve for high.

After the third up card has been dealt, your staying requirements depend on what sort of high and low hands seem to be developing around the board. Usually, low fourflushes and bobtails should be played all the way. The big trap, at this point in the game, is two low pairs. They are difficult to improve, and will not normally hold up without improvement against several active opponents.

In five-card forms, the dealer has an even bigger advantage than in six- and seven-card forms. See Little Squeeze for a full discussion.

A number of carding problems develop from time to time in all forms of substitution. For example, you may have a draw to either a high flush or a low hand, as when you hold (♦A)/♣5-6-7-J in Little Squeeze. Familiarity with the tables in Part Two, pages 108–117, will help in such situations, but you should also consider the cards that show around the board as well as the players against you. There's no need to draw for a 7-6-5 if you're pretty sure that another player already holds a smoother 7, as when he shows (?)/A-2-3-7, bets, and holds pat.

When you have a reasonable choice, take your substitution card down. When you hold (2)/3-4-2-6, for example, you would be foolish to substitute for the exposed deuce when you could just as easily take a new hole card. But when you're playing for high it's often wise, at least from a defensive viewpoint, to take an up card in good tight play. Such a case occurs when you hold a hand like (2)/A-A-5-Q. Discard either the 5 or the queen, depending on the up cards you have seen around the board. If you discard the deuce, everyone will know that you did not have two pairs or trip aces, and bets may be forthcoming from players who hold two pairs, or from opponents who, detecting a soft spot, run a bluff on something like (8)/7-8-9-10.

SUDDEN DEATH

This aptly named game is Five-Card Stud—played low. The requirements for staying in on the go are two low cards. Before you play at all, however, remember that catching any pair or any high card is "sudden death." If you do play the game, stay in as long as you continue to catch low cards that don't pair you, or as long as you can beat what you see around the board.

When you catch a court card on the end, weigh the odds carefully before you fold against a single opponent. When he holds (?)/2-3-4-5, his hole card could pair one of his up cards. Do not be too suspicious of his deuce or trey, because he would probably have folded if he had paired so early. Since he played all the way, he probably has a low card in the hole and there is a good chance that the 5 spiked him, especially if none of the 5's have been exposed around the board. So, in limit poker you may have a good gamble on an end-bet call even if you catch a king or spike deuces. But when your opponent catches a queen on the end and you catch a king, fold fast. His queen beats your king and surely did not pair him, since he wouldn't have played on a queen in the hole.

Even when played with low limits, this game is too much of a gamble for the conservative player, and the really tight player couldn't pick a hole card out of the deck that would give him a decided advantage over the rest of the players at the table. I've known players who folded on this game without even looking at their hole cards, and some who even refuse to ante for it. The complete player will hazard a hand of Sudden Death every now and then in a social dealer's choice session—but he will prefer a game that will give him more advantage at less risk.

SUPER SEVEN–CARD STUD LOW

Here's a good one from *Oswald Jacoby on Poker*: "This is an invention of my own which is extremely effective in stirring up action when there are only a few players. To start with, each player is dealt five cards face down. He now discards two cards and turns one up whereupon play proceeds in the same manner as in plain Seven-Card Low.

"In this game you can be practically certain that everyone who stays has two perfect cards in the hole. Now, if another perfect card is dealt to a player, there is a good chance that it will pair him, whereas, if he is dealt a good low card such as an 8 or 9 [in the seventy-five scale], you can be certain that he has improved.

"Thus, suppose your final hand is a 10 low. Your opponent, who started with a 7 up and has drawn a 9, 8, and king, surely had made a 9 low without counting his seventh card. On the other hand, if he had drawn a 4, 3, and king, it would be quite likely that at least one of those two low cards had paired him and your ten low might easily win the pot."

TAKE IT OR LEAVE IT

Also called Shove 'em Along, Hilo Picalo, Option Poker, and Selecto, this game is played high-low. Each player receives one down card. Then one card is turned up in the center. The first player to the dealer's left has the option of taking the center card, or the top card off the deck. If he elects to take the center card, a new card is turned up and the next player has the option of taking it or the top card off the deck. When the first player elects to take the top card, then the center card remains unchanged until some player does choose to take it. When the dealer elects to take a card off the deck, the center card is burned. When the dealer elects to take the center card, another one is not turned until after a betting interval.

At the end of the hand, each active player has one down card and four up cards, as in Five-Card Stud. But of course the hands run much higher in Take It or Leave It, because of the options.

In most cases, it's easy to tell early in the hand whether a player is shooting for high or low. When anyone elects to take a king, for example, he's probably got another one in the hole and is surely going high. When one takes a deuce and has a trey showing, he's going low.

As in most other high-low games, the low hands have the advantage. Unless you pair aces, kings, or queens on the first two cards, play only with a low card in the hole. Get out if you bust your low hand, unless you make a pair on the last card and have reason to believe that you can back in for high money or else won't have any opposition for low.

When you do shoot for high from the outset, you may have to do a little intercepting on your options. You have, for example, (A)/A-2-2 and a king is in the center. A player on your left holds (?)/K-8-Q-9 and you are certain that his hole card is a king because he elected to take his exposed king from the center. In this case, you should take the king to keep him from getting it. Thus, when you are playing high, it is to your advantage to have the other high players to your left. Also—no matter whether you are playing high or low—it is to your advantage to have on your right players who are going the opposite way.

In some circles, the players must pay a penalty if they reject the center card. If the penalty is higher than the minimum bet, get out on the first round if the center card doesn't help your hand. With a low penalty, pay it and draw off the deck whenever you hold a very good low hole card (preferably an ace).

Also see Push.

TELEPHONE
See Cincinnati Liz.

TENNESSEE
See Cincinnati.

TEXAS TECH

Also called Double-Barreled Shotgun and Wild Annie, this game combines the roll 'em back feature of Anaconda with Shotgun. Each player receives three down cards. First betting interval. Another down card. Second betting interval. Another (fifth) down card. Third betting interval. Then each active player can draw to his hand. Fourth betting interval. At this point, each active player arranges his cards to roll 'em back. First roll. Fifth betting interval. Second roll. Sixth betting interval. Third roll. Seventh betting interval. Fourth roll. Eighth betting interval. Showdown. At the end of the roll 'em back phase, each active player has one down card and four up cards, as in Five-Card Stud.

In Shotgun, I recommend that you play only high cards to straights and flushes because it is too expensive to shoot for these hands unless they hold potential for high pairs. The situation is a little different in Texas Tech. It's still expensive to play for straights and flushes, but when you do connect on one you can make a bundle (or lose one!) during the roll 'em back betting intervals.

The staying requirements for the first three cards include a high pair or potential straights and flushes. After the draw, fold any hand that you aren't prepared to play all the way. That is, fold anything lower than high triplets. The only two-pair hand even worth considering is aces up. Turn up an ace on the second and fourth roll 'em back intervals. A pair of aces makes a good scare hand; consequently, it's usually cheaper to see a hand through, or to win by bluffery, when your second up card is an ace.

Texas Tech is often played high-low. As usual, the low hands have all the advantage. But don't start the roll 'em back phase with any hand higher than seventy-four (based on the California scale). The exceptions include medium low hands that are also straights and flushes.

THREE–CARD MONTE

Similar to an old English game called Bragg (a forerunner of poker), this three-card game can be played as either draw or stud, and as high, low, or high-low. In the stud version, each player receives one down card. First betting interval. Up card, bet. Up card, bet. Showdown. In the draw version, each player receives three cards down. Bet. Draw. Bet. Showdown.

Four of-a-kind, full houses, and two pairs are impossible in Three-Card Monte. Sets of triplets are the best high hands. Then three-card flushes. Then three-card straights. Then single pairs. Some circles, however, do not recognize three-card straights and flushes.

A pair will usually win high, especially when the flushes and straights are not counted. 4's and 5's are not uncommon for low. In high-low, an ace is a key card, especially in cards speak, because a hand like A-2-5 will swing on one like 2-3-5; on the other hand, it's harder to hit a three-card straight with an A-2 than with 2-3.

333

Each player receives three down cards and three up cards. Treys are wild. Straights and flushes are common in 333. Triplets will sometimes hold up in tight play, where many of the potential straights and flushes are folded before they develop. The staying requirements for conservative play include a wild card or a natural pair on the first three cards.

As in 444, there are several variations in the mechanics of the deal. Some players deal three cards down at the outset. Others deal two down, three up, and one more down. Still others alternate one up and one down. The more conservative players will prefer to see three cards to his hand before the first betting interval.

TOAD–IN–THE–HOLE

See Wild Widow.

TRIPS TO WIN

This version of Jacks is an unusual poker game in that you don't necessarily lose if you get caught bluffing! It is dealt exactly like ordinary Jacks. But it takes triplets to win. After someone opens on a pair of jacks (or better), every active player draws to his hand. There is a betting interval after the draw, but a new deal is required if no one holds triplets or better at the showdown. Once a player drops, he is out until some active player does finally make triplets, no matter how many new deals are required.

The more players that drop out, the harder it becomes to get jack openers and trip winners. Sometimes huge pots are built by accumulative antes and bets. Once the pot does get very large in relation to the maximum bet, players stay in—drawing to anything and calling bluff bets even on busted flushes—until some lucky player does come up with triplets or better.

If you want to play a conservative game of poker, don't become involved in one of these pots unless you have triplets or a shot at a straight or flush at the outset. Remember that it's just as hard to trip aces as deuces, so that the higher pairs don't have too much advantage over the short (unless both happen to trip at the same time). When you do play the game, always split two pairs and draw three cards to the highest pair. This will increase your chances of making triplets. Never hold a kicker to a pair—unless you plan to run a bluff.

TULSA

See Hold Me.

TWIN BEDS

Each player receives five cards face down. Then two rows of five cards each are dealt face down in the widow, as in Bedsprings. These cards will be turned up one at the time, alternating from row to row, with a betting interval following each turn. When all the widow cards are up, each active player may use cards from one five-card row or the other (but not from both) in his poker hand.

Winning hands run a little higher than in Cincinnati for both high and low. The playing requirements are pretty much the same as in Cincinnati, but should be somewhat more conservative because Twin Beds has twice as many betting intervals. Never play for flushes in Twin Beds.

TWO AND TWENTY–TWO

This numbers game is played exactly like Seven and Twenty-Seven except that the players go for a total of 2 or 22 instead of 7 or 27. Generally, the text for Seven and Twenty-Seven will apply here.

The big difference is that very good low hands are harder to come by. Therefore, bluffery and positional betting on a sorry low hand like (8)/K are much more likely to succeed in Two and Twenty-

Two than in Seven and Twenty-Seven. Also remember than an ace has more importance, since a hand like (10)/A can possibly win both ways, if you can persuade all the other low hands to either get out or shoot for high. Two aces make the perfect hand—2 and 22.

Generally, the best bet is a pat low hand, as in Seven and Twenty-Seven. But the half is by far a stronger hand in Two and Twenty-Two because only two aces make a perfect pat low. Aces can combine only 6 ways to form a pair in Two and Twenty-Two, whereas 48 combinations can make a pat seven in Seven and Twenty-Seven. (There are 16 combinations of 5-2 that will make a perfect seven; 16 combinations of 6-A; and 16 combinations of 4-3.) Consequently, it is seldom advisable to hit the half in Two and Twenty-Two.

UTAH
See Cincinnati.

V–8 SPECIAL
A widow game similar to Cincinnati Liz. Each player receives five cards face down. Then nine cards are turned up in the widow, in the shape of a V. The bottom card of the V, and all like it, is wild. When played high-low, as it usually is, a player can use one side of the V for high and the other for low. The discussion under Cincinnati Liz will apply to V-8 Special.

WIDOW POKER
A form of poker that is neither stud nor draw. One or more cards are turned face up in the middle of the table. Some or all of these cards may be counted in your best poker hand. The more popular widow games include Cincinnati, Hold Me, Bedsprings, and Southern Cross.

The principles of widow poker were discussed at length in Chapter 8. Also see the discussions under Cincinnati and Hold Me.

WILD ANNIE
See Texas Tech.

WILD WIDOW
Also called Pig-in-the-Poke, Toad-in-the-Hole, and, sometimes, Spit-in-the-Ocean, this is a draw game in which a card turned face

up in the center designates the wild card. But the widow card itself does *not* work in each player's hand. In other words, there are only three wild cards.

There are minor variations in the deal, but ultimately each player receives five cards in his hand (as compared to four in Spit). The mathematics and strategy are pretty much the same as for Deuces Wild, except that the hands will not average out quite as high as in Deuces. The staying requirements can therefore be relaxed slightly.

In one version of Wild Widow, each player receives four down cards as in Spit. After a betting interval, each active player receives another down card. Then the final betting interval and showdown occur, without an option to draw. A pair of aces or kings are worth a call during the first betting interval and may win without improvement, especially if you hold a wild card. Raise on any set of triplets.

Players used to Spit-in-the-Ocean often misread their hands in Wild Widow. Look closely, and remember that the widow card merely designates the wild rank and does not work in your poker hand.

WIN TWO

A draw game (or series) in which you have to win two hands to get the pot. Win Two can be played like Jacks, Guts, Blind Tiger, and so on. Often the pots grow quite large before one player is lucky enough to make his second win, so that the odds become right for draws to inside straights, short pairs, and even monkey flushes— *if* you have already won a hand.

The way to play this game conservatively is to drop out of the series if you don't win the first hand or have a very good prospect of winning the second. But when you do win the first hand, you have a tremendous advantage over the other players because you have to win only one more whereas any one of your opponents has to win two.

WOOLWORTH

A Seven-Card Stud form with 5's and 10's wild. The playing requirements and strategy are pretty much the same as for Baseball.

In some circles, the 5's and 10's are penalty cards when dealt up. As in Baseball, the price you pay for these wild cards varies widely from group to group. My advice is that you should not pay heavily for these wild up cards unless you have at least one more in the hole.

Woolworth is sometimes called Five and Ten.

X–MARKS–THE–SPOT

Each player receives five cards down, as in Southern Cross. Then five cards are dealt into the widow in the shape of a big plus sign. These cards are turned up, one by one, either counterclockwise or clockwise, with a betting interval following each turn. The center card is turned up last; it, and all like it, is wild. If you hold 2-5-J-Q-A, for example, and

A

2 2 Q

10

turn up in the widow, you have five aces.

My objection to X-Marks-the-Spot is that you have to see too many bets before you know the rank of the wild cards. Whenever you play anything less than high triplets down, you're gambling. The game is much better, or more stable, if the wild center card is turned first.

Anyhow, after all the widow cards are turned, only five-of-a-kind makes a really strong hand.

A similar game is called Criss Cross. It is dealt like X-Marks-the-Spot and the center card is still wild. The big difference is that you can play only three widow cards—and they must be in a straight line, either crossways or up and down. If the sample hand above were dealt in Criss Cross, you would not have five aces because the two widow deuces are not aligned with the widow ace. In this particular case, you would have five queens: 2-2-Q in the widow plus the 2-Q among your down cards. Again, the wild center card is usually turned up last. Again, you're gambling if you start playing anything less than high triplets down.

YOU ROLL TWO

See Seven-Card Flip.

ZIG–ZAG

A widow game in the vein of X-Marks-the-Spot and V-8 Special. Each player receives five cards face down. Then 13 cards are turned up in the widow, forming a big Z, such as

2 5 A J Q
     4
   8
  K
J 9 7 3 6

You can play any of the three sets of aligned cards in your best poker hand; that is, you can play the top row, the bottom row, or the diagonal row. The cards (and all like them) at the two zag points of the Z are wild, *except* when a one-eyed jack falls. A one-eyed jack in the widow nullifies the customary wild cards (and all like ⁺hem) but defines a new set. The card (and all like it) immediately preceding the one-eyed jack becomes wild, as well as the card (and all like it) immediately following the one-eyed jack. A complication occurs when a one-eyed jack falls at one or the other of the two zag points of the Z, in which case. . . .

Well, I'd better not finish the text for Zig-Zag, lest Charlie deal it in the next Friday night session! I confess that I made the game up for the benefit of the people in my publisher's office who have to write the poop that goes on the dust jacket of books. I'd like for them to be able to say that Livingston covers poker from A to Z!

Glossary / Index

A: Abbreviation for an ace.

ABC Straight: An A-2-3-4-5 straight.

Able: The player to the dealer's immediate left.

According to Hoyle: By the rules.

Acepots, 122

Acey-Deucey, 154

Action: A catch-all expression that denotes gambling, used in such expressions as, "Where's the action?"

Active Player: A player who has not folded his hand or otherwise forfeited his interest in the pot.

Advertise (bluffery), 34–36

Age: The player to the dealer's immediate left, also called able.

Alternate Straight, 191

Amarillo, 75, 153

Ambigu, 29

Anaconda, 123–127, 167

Announce: Same as Declare (in high-low poker).

Announced Bet: Same as Mouth Bet.

Ante, 16, 27

Arkansas Flush: A fourflush.

As Nas, 29

Australia, 132, 141

Backed Up: Same as Back to Back.

Back In: (1). To call or raise after having checked. (2). To win (or declare) the opposite way from which one had been playing in high-low poker.

Backraise: In most modern poker games, there is a limit to the number of raises permitted (usually three) during each betting interval. A backraise is a nominal raise made to kill, or prevent, a higher raise.

Back to Back: A pair on the first two cards in stud, one up and one down.

Bacon, Francis, 39

Bad Seven (eight, nine, etc.): Same as Rough Seven.

Bait: To advertise. A play made for advertising purposes or to entice a player to bet, call, or raise.

Baker: The second player to the dealer's left.

Bank, Banker: A kitty containing money paid for chips. Usually, one player, called the banker, has charge of such chips.

Baseball, 127–128

Baseball High-Low, 128–129

Bear: A cautious player.

Beat Your Neighbor, 129, 189

Bedsprings, 129–130

Bee Playing Cards, 78, 79

Behind the Log: To play conservatively while substantially ahead in the session.

Belly Strippers, 80–81

Best Flush, 130

Bet in the Blind: To bet without looking at one's cards.

By Me: An expression meaning "I check" or "I pass."

Calamity Jane: The queen of spades.

California, 14

California (game), 135

California Lowball, 66, 133, 162, 165

Call: To put enough chips or cash into the pot to equal a bet or raise.

Calling all Bets: See Play Behind.

Calling Out of Turn, 13

Canadian Stud, 168–169

Cape Horn, 35

Cardano, Gerolamo, 82

Carding: (1). The strategy and mathematics, or both, involved in drawing to one's hand. See Chapter 6. (2). Remembering the cards that have been folded in stud forms.

Card Mechanic, 76–78

Card Memory, 55–57, 142

Cards Speak (high-low), 62–63

Cards Speak for Themselves: The rule in poker that the value of a player's hand is determined not by what he thinks he has or says that he has but by the cards themselves as seen and verified by his opponents.

Carte Blanche: A poker hand that does not contain a face card.

Case Card: The last unexposed card of a particular rank. The term probably came into poker parlance through the game of faro.

Cash Out, Cash In: To convert one's chips to cash, usually when quitting the game.

Casing: Remembering cards that have been dealt.

Castle, Jeffery Lloyd, 163

Catalog Man: A pseudoknowledgeable player who obtains information about cheating devices and techniques not from firsthand experience but from catalogs and gaff supply houses.

Catch: To be dealt a particular card or cards.

that Big Tigers, Little Tigers, Big Dogs, and Little Dogs will be recognized in a particular deal, session, or group. See Special Hands, pages 191–193.

Ceiling Bet (pot limit), 20

Cellar Dealer, 76

C-H, 83

Chances (odds), 91

Charlie: The third player to the dealer's left.

Chase: To draw or play against a superior hand. To send good money after bad.

Check: In effect, a check is a bet of nothing. In the early days of poker, a player had to bet something or drop. Players began making a nominal bet of one chip (or check) when they did not want to throw away their hands and yet did not want to make a large wager on it. Other players started "chipping along" and finally the physical chip, which had proved to be a nuisance, was dropped.

Check and Raise, 14, 15, 46

Check Blind, Check in the Dark: To check without looking at one's hand.

Checking Out of Turn, 13–14

Chicago, 136–137

Chink Ink: Ink used in marking cards.

Chip Along. To call a nominal bet.

Chips: Plastic disks or similar tokens substituted for cash.

Chips Declare, 62–66

Chip the Pot: Same as Cut the Pot.

Cinch Hand: An unbeatable hand, a lock.

Cincinnati, 115, 133–135

Cincinnati Liz, 135

Cincinnati, Ohio, 15

Clinic: A poker game made up mostly of doctors.

Closed Poker, 121, 140

Close to the Chest (belly): Playing tightly.

Floating Game (continued)
moves from place to place, often to avoid cops and robbers.

Flower: A flush.

Flush: A poker hand containing five cards of the same suit. Of the 2,598,-960 possible poker hands, 5,108 are flushes. *See* Rank of Poker Hands.

Fold: To pass or drop out of the hand.

Folding out of Turn, 13

Follow the Queen, 146

Football, 146–147

Fort Griffin, Texas, 17

Forty Niners, 35

Foster, Robert F., 197

Four-Bluff: A bluff made on a busted flush or straight.

Fourflush: (1). Four cards to a flush. (2). A nonstandard hand, 192

Fourflush Stud, 168–169

444, 147

Four-of-a-Kind: A poker hand containing four cards of the same rank. Of the 2,598,960 possible poker hands, 624 are four-of-a-kind. *See* Rank of Poker Hands.

Fours: Four-of-a-kind.

Freak: A wild card or joker.

Freak Hands: Nonstandard poker hands. *See* Special Hands, page 191.

Free Ride: A round of betting in which everyone checks.

Free Wheeler: A player who has lost all his money or chips in Poverty Poker and is allowed to play free until he wins a pot.

Freeze: To draw no more cards in numbers games like Seven and Twenty-Seven.

Freezeout: A session in which a player must quit when he loses his original table stake.

Freezer: A raise made to stop further raising. Some circles allow only three raises; the third raise, if made for a token amount, would be the freezer.

Full Hand: Same as Full House.

Full House: A poker hand containing three-of-a-kind and a pair, such as K-K-K-8-8. Of the 2,598,960 possible poker hands, 3,744 are full houses. *See* Rank of Poker Hands.

Full Table: A poker session in which there is no open seat.

Gaff: A cheater's device or technique. A gaff supply house is a business that traffics in this sort of thing, usually along with legerdemain gear.

Garbage: Undesirable or unplayable cards; discards.

Garbage Pile: Discard pile.

Garcia Cut, 86–87

Garcia, Frank, 81, 86

Go All In: When a player bets all his chips or cash, he is said to go all in. In some circles he can obtain additional funds (if he loses) and continue in the session; in other games he must quit if he loses after having gone all in.

Go One Better: To raise—or re-raise.

Goose: A foolish player.

Go South: (1). To palm cards. (2). To cop chips or money from the pot. (3). To rathole chips-or money. (4). To quit a session while ahead.

Gruesome Twosome, 154

Gut Shot: A draw to an inside straight.

Gut Straight: An inside straight.

Guts to Open, 196–197

Half-Pot Limit, 20

Hand: (1). The cards that are dealt to a player. A poker hand contains five cards, except in two-, three-, and four-card games. In games like Seven-Card Stud, a player selects his best five cards as his poker hand. (2). A particular deal in a session is called a hand, as in "Deal me in for a couple of hands."

Hart, Schaffner, and Marx: Three jacks.

days of poker. Ostensibly, a player could bet anything—money or goods —that he could put on the table or represent by title, deed, or bill of sale. Regardless of who held the best poker hand, a player lost if he could not cover a bet within twenty-four hours. Well, there were no doubt some sessions played in this manner; but, obviously, the ordinary player would not have stood a chance against a millionaire. In "no limit" games, then, the players were probably allowed to call only whatever they could cover of a large bet, which would be close to what we now call table stakes.

Nonstandard Hands: Poker hands that are not universal, but which are recognized in some groups. See Special Hands, pages 191–193.

No Pair: A poker hand containing no pair, no straight, and no flush. Of the 2,598,960 possible poker hands, 1,302,540 are no pair. See Rank of Poker Hands.

One-End Straight: A possible straight that is open only on one end, as A-2-3-4-X. Also called One-Way Straight.

One-Eyed Jacks: The jack of spades and the jack of hearts, both of which are shown in profile on most standard playing cards.

One-Eyes: The jack of spades, jack of hearts, and king of diamonds. See page 169.

One Pair: A poker hand containing two cards of the same rank. Of the 2,598,960 possible poker hands,

1,098,240 are one pair. See Rank of Poker Hands.

One-Way Straight: A one-end straight, such as A-K-Q-J-X.

On the Come: To bet or call before one has made a flush or some such hand.

Open: To make the first bet in a hand of poker.

Open Blind, Open in the Dark: To open without looking at one's cards. See Blind Tiger.

Open-End Straight: A four-card straight that is open on both ends, such as 8-9-10-J. Usually called a bobtail straight.

Openers, Opening Requirements: In draw games like Jacks, a certain ranking hand (or better) is required to open the pot. The minimum rank of hand on which a player may open is called openers.

Open Game: A poker session in which any player may participate if a seat is available.

Open on Anything: Same as Guts to Open.

Open Pair: An exposed pair in stud forms.

Open Seat: An available slot at a poker table. If a game allows a maximum of eight players but has only seven, there is one open seat.

Pack: A deck of playing cards.

Packet: A portion of a deck of playing cards.

Paint: Jacks, queens, and kings in lowball; the term is often used as a verb.

Pair: Two cards of the same rank.

Slick Seven: *See* Rough Seven.

Slow Play: To sandbag or bet moderately on a good hand.

Smooth Seven: *See* Rough Seven.

Social Game: A poker game played among friends and more for pleasure than for financial gain.

Sorts, 80

South Africa, 132, 141

Southern Cross, 191

Special Hands, 22, 145, 191–193

Spider, 83

Spike: To pair up when playing low poker.

Spit Card: The card that is turned up in the widow in Spit-in-the-Ocean.

Spit-in-the-Ocean, 193–195, 206–207

Split Openers, 15. To discard one of a pair of jacks, or other rank of openers, in order to draw for a flush or straight.

Split Pair: A pair in stud forms with one card up and one down.

Split Pot: A pot that is divided by two players in such games as Chicago and high-low.

Spot Card: A 2, 3, 4, 5, 6, 7, 8, 9, or 10—all of which have spots or pips.

Spread, 85–86

Squeeze Out, Sweat Out: To hope for; to peep at one's draw cards in a slow, hopeful manner.

Squeeze Play, 31

Stack: (1). A stack of chips. (2). The total amount of chips or cash that a player has in front of him. (3). To finagle with the deck, in one way or another, in preparation for a crooked deal.

Stake: The amount of cash or chips that one has readily available to play on.

Stand Pat, Play Pat: To draw no cards.

Stay: To call. To remain active in the pot.

Steig, Irwin, 40, 161

Steal a Pot: To win a pot by bluffing.

Stock: The undealt portion of the deck.

Stonewall Jackson: A tight player.

Stormy Weather, 195–196

Straddle, 132

Straight: A poker hand containing five cards in sequence. Of the 2,598,960 possible poker hands, 10,200 are straights. *See* Rank of Poker Hands.

Straight Draw, 196–197

Straight Flush: A poker hand containing five cards in sequence and of the same suit. Of the 2,598,960 possible poker hand, only 40 are straight flushes. *See* Rank of Poker Hands.

Straight Poker, 197

Stranger: A term used in draw poker to denote a card that was drawn to the original hand.

String Bet: A bet made in more than one installment.

Strip Poker, 197

Stud, 72–74, 197–198

Substitution Poker, 121, 198–200

Sudden Death, 200–201

Summertime Hand: A middling hand, especially one that loses.

Sunning the Deck, 80

Super Seven-Card Stud Low, 201

Swag: Winnings.

Sweat Out: To peep at one's cards in a slow, hopeful manner.

Sweeten, Sweeten the Pot: To re-ante or otherwise add chips to a pot that has not been opened.

Swing Hand: A hand that wins both ways in high-low poker.

Table Stakes, 19, 26, 47

Take It or Leave It, 201–202

Takeout, 19

Talon: The deck or undealt portion of it. The discard pile is sometimes called the talon.

Tap: To bet all the chips or money one has in front of him, or to bet enough